UNIT

Edexcel AS | 2

Biology

Development, Plants and the Environment

Mary Jones

D1144382

CITY OF BRISTOL COLLEGE

00163273

S7G   10-08-2009

Jan   7-99

9780340948309   COL

Philip Allan Updates, an imprint of Hodder Education, an Hachette UK company, Market Place, Deddington, Oxfordshire OX15 0SE

Orders

Bookpoint Ltd, 130 Milton Park, Abingdon, Oxfordshire OX14 4SB
tel: 01235 827720
fax: 01235 400454
e-mail: uk.orders@bookpoint.co.uk

Lines are open 9.00 a.m.–5.00 p.m., Monday to Saturday, with a 24-hour message answering service. You can also order through the Philip Allan Updates website: www.philipallan.co.uk

© Philip Allan Updates 2009

ISBN 978-0-340-94830-9

First printed 2009
Impression number 5 4 3 2
Year 2014 2013 2012 2011 2010 2009

All rights reserved; no part of this publication may be reproduced, stored in a retrieval system, or transmitted, in any other form or by any means, electronic, mechanical, photocopying, recording or otherwise without either the prior written permission of Philip Allan Updates or a licence permitting restricted copying in the United Kingdom issued by the Copyright Licensing Agency Ltd, Saffron House, 6–10 Kirby Street, London EC1N 8TS.

This guide has been written specifically to support students preparing for the Edexcel AS Biology Unit 2 examination. The content has been neither approved nor endorsed by Edexcel and remains the sole responsibility of the author.

Typeset by Greenhill Wood Studios
Printed by MPG Books, Bodmin

Hachette UK's policy is to use papers that are natural, renewable and recyclable products and made from wood grown in sustainable forests. The logging and manufacturing processes are expected to conform to the environmental regulations of the country of origin.

Contents

Introduction

■ ■ ■

Content Guidance

■ ■ ■

Questions and Answers

Introduction
About this guide

This book is the second in a series of four, which will help you to prepare for the Edexcel AS and A-level biology examination. It covers **Unit 2: Development, Plants and the Environment**. This is the second of two content-based units that make up the AS biology examination. The other three books in the series cover Units 1, 4 and 5.

This guide has three main sections:
- **Introduction**   This contains an overview of the unit and how it is assessed, some advice on revision and advice on doing the examination.
- **Content Guidance**   This provides a summary of the facts and concepts that you need to know for the Unit 2 examination.
- **Questions and Answers**   This section contains two specimen papers for you to try, each worth 80 marks. There are also two sets of answers for each question, one from a candidate who is likely to get a C grade and another from a candidate who is likely to get an A grade.

It's entirely up to you how you use this book. We suggest you start by reading through this Introduction, which will give you some suggestions about how you can improve your knowledge and skills in biology and about good ways of revising. It also gives you some pointers into how to do well in the examination. The Content Guidance will be especially useful when you are revising, as will the Questions and Answers.

The specification

It is a good idea to have your own copy of the Edexcel biology specification. It's you who is going to take this examination, not your teacher, and so it is your responsibility to make sure you know as much about the exam as possible. You can download a copy free from **www.edexcel.org.uk**.

The AS examination is made up of three units:
- Unit 1 Lifestyle, Transport, Genes and Health
- Unit 2 Development, Plants and the Environment
- Unit 3 Practical Biology and Research Skills

This book covers Unit 2, and the first book in the series covers Unit 1. There is no book for Unit 3, because this is based on practical work that you will do in your biology classes.

Concept-led or context-led?

There are two ways of working through the specification, and your teacher will be able to tell you which one you are following. He or she may be taking a context-led approach, in which you start with a context such as a person having a heart attack, and then look at biological facts, principles and concepts associated with this. Or you may be following a concept-led approach, in which you start with the biological facts, principles and concepts and then look at how these can be applied to particular contexts.

In the end, there is not much difference — you need to learn all the biology whichever way you approach it! In this book we have followed a concept-led approach, but you'll find it easy to follow, whichever approach you have been taking in your biology course.

Unit 2 content

The content of each unit is clearly set out in the specification. Unit 2 has two topics:
• The voice of the genome
• Biodiversity and natural resources

The voice of the genome looks at the detailed structures of an animal cell, as an example of a eukaryotic cell, and of a prokaryotic cell. The functions of organelles involved with protein synthesis and export in an animal cell are explained. The topic moves on to consider mitosis and the cell cycle, and how you can prepare a piece of plant root to observe cells in various stages of the cell cycle. The roles of meiosis are also considered, although you do not need to know details of its stages for this Unit. The structures and functions of mammalian gametes are covered, and also the processes involved in fertilisation in mammals and flowering plants.

We then look at stem cells — what they are, what they do and their potential importance in future treatments of diseases. This leads us to the idea of differentiation, and what this involves. Finally, the relationship between phenotype, genotype and environment is considered.

Biodiversity and natural resources concentrates largely on plants to begin with. We look at the ultrastructure of plant cells, and relate the structure and function of starch and cellulose to their functions in these cells. Some of the uses that we make of plant fibres and starch are dealt with, including an experiment that you can do to investigate the tensile strength of fibres. Other practical work you need to be familiar with includes the investigation of plant mineral deficiencies using culture solutions, and testing for antimicrobial properties of plant extracts. Plants are important sources of drugs, and we look at old and new methods of testing their efficacy and safety.

The rest of the topic deals with biodiversity — what it is and how we can measure it. The ways in which organisms become adapted to their environment, through natural selection, are discussed. Conservation is considered, especially relating to the roles of zoos and seedbanks.

Unit 2 assessment

Unit 2 is assessed in an examination lasting 1 hour 15 minutes. The questions are all structured — that is, they are broken up into several parts, with spaces in which you write your answers. There are 80 marks available on the paper.

What is assessed?

It's easy to forget that your examination isn't just testing what you *know* about biology — it's also testing your *skills*. It's difficult to overemphasise how important these are.

The Edexcel examination tests three different assessment objectives (AOs). The following table gives a breakdown of the proportion of marks awarded to knowledge and to skills in the AS examination:

Assessment objective	Outline of what is tested	Percentage of marks
AO1	Knowledge and understanding of science and of How Science Works	30–34
AO2	Applications of knowledge and understanding of science and of How Science Works	34–40
AO3	How Science Works	28

AO1 is about remembering and understanding all the biological facts and concepts you have covered in this unit. AO2 is about being able to *use* these facts and concepts in new situations. The examination paper will include questions that contain unfamiliar contexts or sets of data, which you will need to interpret in the light of the biological knowledge you have. When you are revising, it is important that you try to develop your ability to do this, as well as just learning the facts.

AO3 is about How Science Works. Note that this comes into AO1 and AO2 as well. A science subject such as biology is not just a body of knowledge. Scientists do research to find out how things around them work, and new research continues to find out new things all the time. Sometimes new research means that we have to change our ideas. For example, not all that long ago people were encouraged to eat lots of eggs and drink lots of milk, because it was thought to be 'healthy'. Now we know we need to take care not to eat too many animal-based fats, because new research has found links between a fatty diet and heart disease.

How Science Works is about developing theories and models in biology, and testing them. It involves doing experiments to test hypotheses, and analysing the results to determine whether the hypothesis is supported or disproved. You need to appreciate why science does not always give us clear answers to the questions we ask, and how we can design good experiments whose results we can trust.

Scientific language

Throughout your biology course, and especially in your examination, it is important to use clear and correct biological language. Scientists take great care to use language precisely. If doctors or researchers do not use exactly the correct word when communicating with someone, then what they are saying could easily be misinterpreted. Biology has a huge number of specialist terms (probably more than any other subject you can choose to study at AS) and it is important that you learn them and use them. Your everyday conversational language, or what you read in the newspaper or hear on the radio, is often not the kind of language required in a biology examination. Be precise and careful in what you write, so that an examiner cannot possibly misunderstand you.

Revision

There are many different ways of revising, and what works well for you may not be as suitable for someone else. Have a look at the suggestions below and try some of them out.

- **Revise continuously.** Don't think that revision is something you do just before the exam. Life is much easier if you keep revision ticking along all through your biology course. Find 15 minutes a day to look back over work you did a few weeks ago, to keep it fresh in your mind. You will find this helpful when you come to start your intensive revision.

- **Understand it.** Research has shown that we learn things much more easily if our brain recognises that they are important to us and that they make sense to us. Before you try to learn a topic, make sure that you understand it. If you don't, ask a friend or a teacher, find a different textbook in which to read about it, or look it up on the internet. Work at it until you feel you have got it sorted and then try to learn it.

- **Make your revision active.** Just reading your notes or a textbook won't do any harm, but it won't do all that much good, either. Your brain only puts things into its long-term memory if it thinks they are important, so you need to convince it that they are. You can do this by making your brain *do* something with what you are trying to learn. So, if you are revising a table comparing the structure of prokaryotic and eukaryotic cells, try rewriting it as bullet points. If you are revising independent assortment from a flow diagram, try rewriting it as a paragraph of text. Some people like drawing spider diagrams. You will learn much more by constructing your own table, flow diagram or set of bullet points than just trying to remember one that someone else has constructed.

- **Fair shares for all.** Don't always start your revision in the same place. If you always start at the beginning of the course, then you will learn a lot about cells but not much about biodiversity. Make sure each part of the specification gets its fair share of your attention.

- **Plan your time.** You may find it helpful to draw up a revision planner, setting out what you will revise and when. Even if you don't stick to it, it will give you a framework that you can refer to — if you get behind with it, you can rewrite the next bits of the plan to squeeze in the topics you haven't yet covered.

- **Keep your concentration.** It's often said that it is best to revise in short periods, say 20 minutes or half an hour. This is true for many people, if they find it difficult to concentrate for longer than that. But there are others who actually find it better to settle down for a much longer period of time — even several hours — and really get into their work and stay concentrated without interruptions. Find out which works best for you. It may be different at different times of day. Maybe you can only concentrate well for 30 minutes in the morning, but are able to get lost in your work for several hours in the evening.

- **Don't assume you know it.** The topics where exam candidates are least likely to do well are, strangely, the ones that they have already learned something about at GCSE. This is probably because if you think you already know something then you give that a low priority when you are revising. It's important to remember that what you knew for GCSE is probably not detailed enough for AS.

The examination

Once you are in the examination room, at least you can stop worrying about whether or not you've done enough revision. The important thing now is to make the best use of the knowledge and understanding and skills that you have managed to get into your brain.

Time

You will have 75 minutes to answer questions worth 80 marks. That gives you almost 1 minute per mark. When you are trying out a test question, time yourself. Are you working too fast? Or are you taking too long? Get used to what it feels like to work at just over a-mark-a-minute rate.

It's not a bad idea to spend one of those minutes just skimming through the exam paper before you start writing. Maybe one of the questions looks as though it is going to need a bit more of your time than the others. If so, make sure you leave a little bit of extra time for it.

Read the question carefully

That sounds obvious, but candidates lose large numbers of marks by not doing it.

- There is often vital information at the start of the question that you'll need in order to answer the questions themselves. Don't just jump straight to the first place where there are answer lines and start writing. Start reading at the beginning! Examiners are usually careful not to give you unnecessary information, so if it is there it is probably needed. You may like to use a highlighter to pick out any particularly important bits of information in the question.

- Do look carefully at the command words (the ones right at the start of the question) and do what they say. For example, if you are asked to *explain* something then you won't get many marks — perhaps none at all — if you *describe* it instead. You can find all these words in an appendix near the end of the specification document.

Depth and length of answer

The examiners will give you two useful guidelines about how much you need to write.

- **The number of marks.** Obviously, the more marks the more information you need to give. If there are 2 marks, then you'll need to give two different pieces of information in order to get both of them. If there are 5 marks, you'll need to write much more.

- **The number of lines.** This isn't such a useful guideline as the number of marks, but it can still help you to know how much to write. If you find your answer won't fit on the lines, then you probably haven't focused sharply enough on the question. The best answers are short and precise.

Writing, spelling and grammar

The examiners are testing your biology knowledge and skills, not your English skills. Still, if they can't understand what you have written then they can't give you any marks. It is your responsibility to communicate clearly — don't scribble so fast that the examiner cannot read what you have written.

In general, incorrect spellings are not penalised. If the examiner knows what you are trying to say then he or she will give you credit. However, if your wrongly spelt word could be confused with another, then you won't be given the mark. For example, if you write 'meitosis', then the examiner can't know whether you mean meiosis or mitosis, so you'll be marked wrong.

Like spelling, bad grammar isn't taken into account. Once again, though, if it is so bad that the examiner cannot understand you, then you won't get marks. A common problem is to use the word 'it' in such as way that the examiner can't be certain what 'it' refers to. A good general rule is never to use this word in an exam answer.

Content
Guidance

This section of the guide summarises what you need to know for the Unit 2 test. It is divided into two topics:

(1) The voice of the genome

- Structure of prokaryotic cells and animal cells
- The cell cycle and mitosis
- Meiosis and fertilisation
- Stem cells
- Effects of genotype and environment on phenotype

(2) Biodiversity and natural resources

- Structure of plant cells and tissues
- Starch and cellulose
- Making use of materials from plants
- Natural selection and adaptation
- Classification
- Zoos and seed banks

The voice of the genome

Cell structure

All living organisms are made up of cells, and a cell can be thought of as the basic unit of living things. There are two basic types of cells — **prokaryotic** cells and **eukaryotic** cells. Prokaryotic cells are found in bacteria and archaea. Eukaryotic cells are found in animals, plants and fungi.

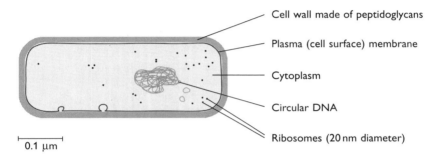

Cell wall made of peptidoglycans

Plasma (cell surface) membrane

Cytoplasm

Circular DNA

Ribosomes (20 nm diameter)

0.1 µm

Structure of a prokaryotic cell

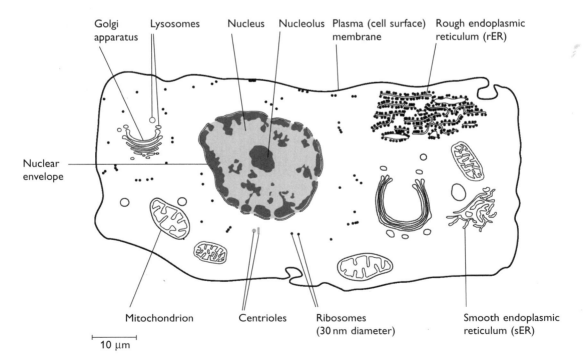

Golgi apparatus   Lysosomes   Nucleus   Nucleolus   Plasma (cell surface) membrane   Rough endoplasmic reticulum (rER)

Nuclear envelope

Mitochondrion   Centrioles   Ribosomes (30 nm diameter)   Smooth endoplasmic reticulum (sER)

10 µm

Structure of an animal cell — an example of a eukaryotic cell

Comparison of prokaryotic and eukaryotic cells

Prokaryotic cell	Eukaryotic cell
No nucleus or nuclear envelope	Nucleus surrounded by envelope (two membranes)
DNA in the form of a single circular molecule	DNA as several linear molecules, each forming a chromosome
Plasmids (small circular pieces of DNA) usually present	No plasmids
Ribosomes 20 nm diameter	Ribosomes 30 nm diameter
No endoplasmic reticulum or Golgi apparatus	Endoplasmic reticulum and Golgi apparatus present
Cell wall always present, made of cross-linked peptidoglycans	Cell wall present in plant cells and fungal cells; made of cellulose in plants and various substances in fungi
No cytoskeleton	Cytoskeleton of microtubules and microfilaments
No mitochondria or plastids	Mitochondria usually present; plastids (chloroplasts and amyloplasts) often present in plant cells

Functions of the rER and Golgi apparatus

Proteins that are to be exported from a cell — for example extracellular enzymes — are made on ribosomes attached to the rough endoplasmic reticulum. Amino acids are strung together into a long chain on the ribosome and joined together by peptide bonds. As the chain forms, it is fed through the membrane of the endoplasmic reticulum so that the protein ends up inside the space (cisternum) between the endoplasmic reticulum membranes.

Part of the cisternum, with the protein molecules inside it, breaks off to form a membrane-bound vesicle. This moves towards the Golgi apparatus. The vesicles fuse to the outer (convex) face of the Golgi apparatus.

Inside the Golgi apparatus, the protein molecules are modified, for example by having carbohydrate groups added to them to produce glycoproteins.

Vesicles containing these modified proteins break away from the inner (concave) face of the Golgi apparatus. The vesicles travel to the cell surface membrane, with which they fuse. Their membranes become part of the cell surface membrane and their contents — the proteins — are deposited outside the cell.

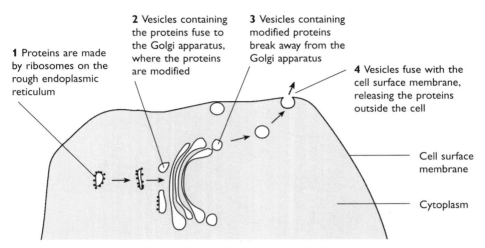

1 Proteins are made by ribosomes on the rough endoplasmic reticulum

2 Vesicles containing the proteins fuse to the Golgi apparatus, where the proteins are modified

3 Vesicles containing modified proteins break away from the Golgi apparatus

4 Vesicles fuse with the cell surface membrane, releasing the proteins outside the cell

Cell surface membrane

Cytoplasm

Formation and secretion of extracellular enzymes

Tissues, organs and systems

Many organisms made of eukaryotic cells (animals, plants and fungi) are multicellular. They generally contain many different types of cells, each specialised to carry out a particular set of functions. For example, your body contains nerve cells (neurones), muscle cells, bone cells, red blood cells and many other cell types.

Cells of a particular type often group together to form a **tissue**. For example, the heart wall is made up of cardiac muscle tissue. Artery walls contain smooth muscle tissue and elastic tissue.

The heart and an artery are examples of **organs**. They are each made up of several different tissues, which work together to carry out the particular function of that organ.

Organs also work together. For example, the heart, arteries, veins and capillaries are all part of the circulatory **system**, whose function is to transport substances around the body.

Cell division

A multicellular organism begins as a single cell. That cell divides repeatedly to produce all the cells in the adult organism.

Mitosis and the cell cycle

The type of cell division involved in growth is called **mitosis**. Mitosis is also involved in asexual reproduction, in which a single parent gives rise to genetically identical offspring.

As an organism grows, many of its cells go through a continuous cycle of growth and mitotic division called the **cell cycle**.

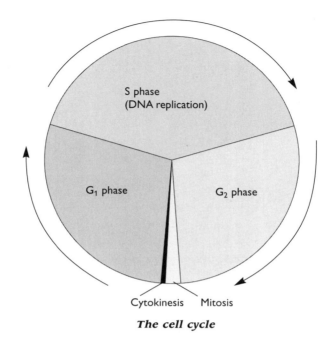

The cell cycle

For most of the cell cycle, in the G_1 and G_2 phases, the cell continues with its normal activities. It also grows, as the result of the production of new molecules of proteins and other substances, which increase the quantity of cytoplasm in the cell.

DNA replication takes place in the S phase, so that there are two identical copies of each DNA molecule in the nucleus. Each DNA molecule forms one chromosome, so after replication is complete each chromosome is made of two identical DNA molecules. They are called **chromatids** and they remain joined together at a point called the **centromere**.

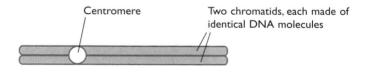

A chromosome before cell division

During mitosis, the two chromatids split apart and are moved to opposite ends of the cell. A new nuclear envelope then forms around each group. These two nuclei each contain a complete set of DNA molecules identical to those in the original (parent) cell. Mitosis produces two genetically identical nuclei from one parent nucleus.

After mitosis is complete, the cell usually divides into two, with one of the new nuclei in each of the two new cells. These two daughter cells are genetically identical to each other and their parent cell.

Prophase

- The chromosomes condense
- The centrioles duplicate
- The centriole pairs move towards each pole
- The spindle begins to form

Metaphase

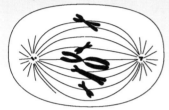

- The nuclear envelope disappears
- The centriole pairs are at the poles
- The spindle is completely formed
- The chromosomes continue to condense
- The microtubules of the spindle attach to the centromeres of the chromosomes
- The microtubules pull on the centromeres, arranging them on the equator

Anaphase

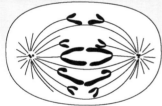

- The links between sister chromatids break
- The centromeres of sister chromatids move apart, pulled by the microtubules of the spindle

Telophase

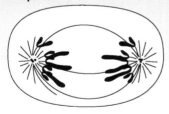

- Sister chromatids (now effectively separate chromosomes) reach opposite poles

Cytokinesis

- The chromosomes decondense
- Nuclear envelopes appear around the chromosomes at each pole
- The spindle disappears
- The cell divides into two cells, by infolding of the plasma membrane in animal cells, or by formation of a new cell wall and plasma membrane in plants

Mitosis and cytokinesis

Making a root tip squash

A good place to find cells going through the cell cycle is just behind the root tip of a young plant. To enable you to see the chromosomes, you need to:

- squash the root so that the cells are spread out in a single layer;
- stain the DNA so that the chromosomes show up clearly when you observe the cells through a microscope. There are various ways of doing this, for example by using a red stain called acetic orcein, which makes DNA red.

Take a young root tip and cut off the end — you want just the 5 mm nearest to the tip. Put your root tip into a small glass container and cover it with acetic orcein stain, mixed with a little $1.0\,mol\,dm^{-3}$ hydrochloric acid. Warm it gently for a few minutes. This will break the cells apart, making it easier to squash the root at the next stage. The stain will make the DNA look red.

Now put the stained root tip onto the centre of a microscope slide. Cut off the end 2 mm and throw this away. Put another couple of drops of acetic orcein onto the part still left on the slide.

Put a coverslip over the root tip on the slide, and wrap the central part of the slide in some filter paper. Very gently, repeatedly tap on the filter paper above the coverslip with the blunt end of a pencil. You are trying to squash the root tip — without breaking the coverslip! Unwrap and check progress every now and then. Aim to get the root tip cells spread out as much as possible, but still in the same relative positions as they were to start with. You can add a bit more stain if it gets too dry.

When you are happy with your root tip squash, hold the slide over a Bunsen flame with your fingers for a few seconds — holding it with your fingers will stop you letting it get too hot. This is critical! It is very easy to overdo it, which will make the chromosomes disintegrate. Now you can look at the slide under the microscope. You should be able to see cells in various stages of mitosis.

Meiosis and gamete production

A few cells in the body — some of those in the testes and ovaries — are able to divide by another type of division, called **meiosis**. Meiosis involves two divisions (not one as in mitosis), so four daughter cells are formed. Meiosis produces four new cells with:

- only half the number of chromosomes as the parent cell
- different combinations of genes from each other and from the parent cell

In animals and flowering plants, meiosis produces **gametes**.

In a human, body cells are **diploid**, containing two complete sets of chromosomes. Meiosis produces gametes that are **haploid**, containing one complete set of chromosomes.

Before meiosis begins, DNA replication takes place exactly as it does before mitosis. However, in the early stages of meiosis, homologous chromosomes (the two 'matching' chromosomes in a nucleus) pair up.

Remember that each chromosome in a homologous pair carries genes for the same characteristics at the same locus. The alleles of the genes on the two chromosomes may be the same or different.

During meiosis, as the two homologous chromosomes lie side by side, their chromatids form links called **chiasmata** (singular: chiasma) with each other. When they move apart, a piece of chromatid from one chromosome may swap places with the other one. This is called **crossing over**. It results in each chromosome having different combinations of alleles from those it had before.

 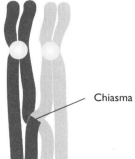 

Chiasma

Homologous pair
of chromosomes

Pieces of each chromatid have
swapped places, resulting in
new combinations of alleles

Crossing over in meiosis

Another feature of meiosis that results in the shuffling of alleles — and therefore genetic variation — is **independent assortment**. During the first division of meiosis, the pairs of homologous chromosomes line up on the equator before being pulled to opposite ends of the cell. Each pair behaves independently from every other pair, so there are many different combinations that can end up together. The diagram shows the different combinations you can get with just two pairs of chromosomes. In a human, there are 23 pairs, so there is a huge number of different possibilities.

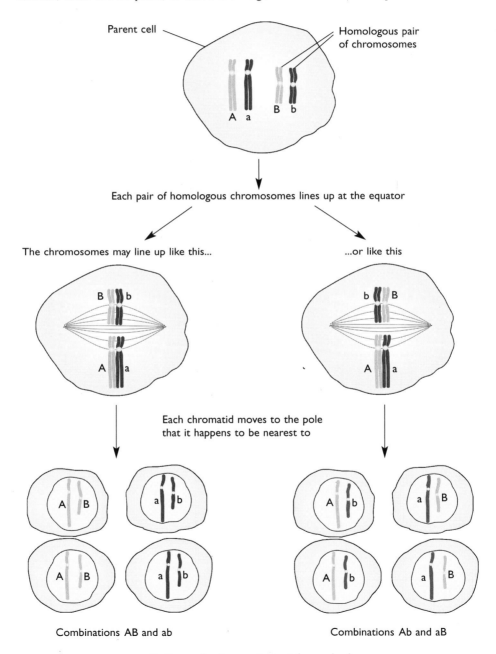

Independent assortment in meiosis

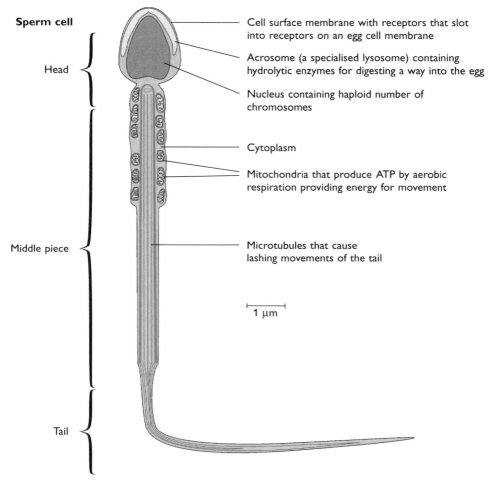

Sperm cell

Head

Middle piece

Tail

Cell surface membrane with receptors that slot into receptors on an egg cell membrane

Acrosome (a specialised lysosome) containing hydrolytic enzymes for digesting a way into the egg

Nucleus containing haploid number of chromosomes

Cytoplasm

Mitochondria that produce ATP by aerobic respiration providing energy for movement

Microtubules that cause lashing movements of the tail

1 μm

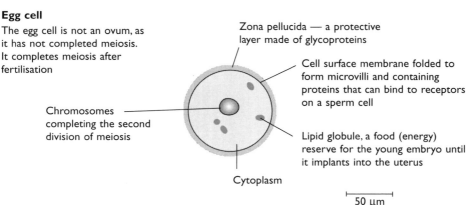

Egg cell

The egg cell is not an ovum, as it has not completed meiosis. It completes meiosis after fertilisation

Zona pellucida — a protective layer made of glycoproteins

Cell surface membrane folded to form microvilli and containing proteins that can bind to receptors on a sperm cell

Chromosomes completing the second division of meiosis

Lipid globule, a food (energy) reserve for the young embryo until it implants into the uterus

Cytoplasm

50 μm

Mammalian gametes

Fertilisation in a mammal

Mammals have internal fertilisation. A liquid called semen, which contains sperm, is introduced into the vagina of a female mammal. The sperm swim towards the oviducts, where they may meet an egg.

The receptors on the cell surface membrane of the sperm cell lock into proteins in the cell surface membrane of the egg cell. This sets off a chain of events that results in the acrosome of the sperm cell releasing its hydrolytic enzymes. These digest the zona pellucida.

While this is happening, the egg responds to the binding of the sperm with its membrane by releasing specialised lysosomes called **cortical granules** into the zona pellucida. These causes changes in the protein molecules in the zona pellucida, altering its structure so that no more sperm can penetrate it. The altered zona pellucida is called a **fertilisation membrane**.

The chromosomes of the egg cell now complete meiosis. However, only one new complete cell is formed — the rest of the chromosomes, instead of forming nuclei in new cells, are 'discarded' and form a tiny, useless object called a **polar body**. So the egg now has one complete set of chromosomes, just as the sperm cell does.

The chromosomes of the sperm join those of the egg. This is the point at which fertilisation happens — it is the fusion of the nuclei of the two gametes. The cell is now diploid, and it is called a **zygote**. This cell is how every young mammal begins. It divides over and over again to eventually form a complete organism.

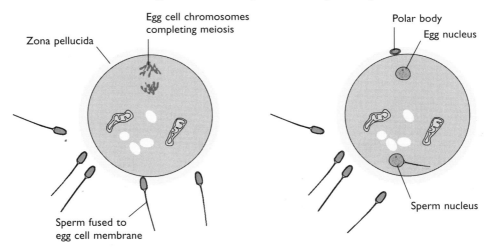

1 A sperm cell digests a path through the zona pellucida using enzymes from its acrosome, and binds to the cell surface membrane of the egg cell. The zona pellucida changes its structure and prevents any more sperm penetrating it.

2 The chromosomes of the egg cell complete meiosis, forming an egg nucleus and a polar body. The sperm nucleus then combines with the egg nucleus.

Fertilisation in a human

Fertilisation in a flowering plant

The flowers of a plant are its sexual reproduction organs. Many species of plants are hermaphrodite — one plant makes both male gametes and female gametes.

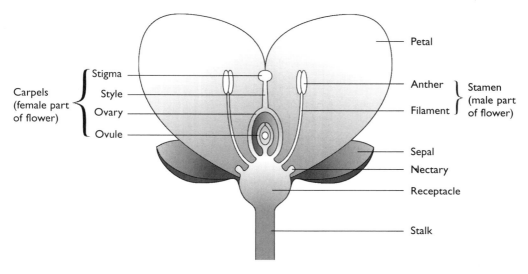

Structure of a flower

In a flowering plant, the male gametes are found inside the **pollen grains**. Each pollen grain contains two haploid nuclei. One is called the **tube nucleus**. The other is the **generative nucleus**, and this will form the male gametes.

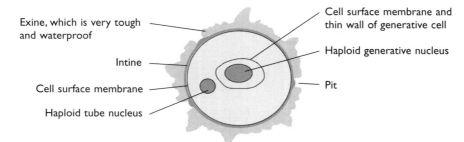

A pollen grain

Pollen grains are carried from one flower to another by insects, birds or the wind. The pollen grain is left on the **stigma** of a flower. This is called **pollination**. If the stigma is the same species as the pollen grain, and if it is ripe, it secretes substances that stimulate the pollen grain to germinate. An area in the tough outer covering breaks down, and a tube grows out. The generative nucleus divides by mitosis to form two male gametes.

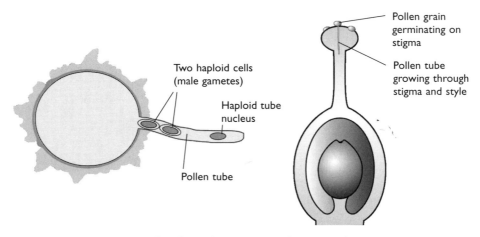

Germination of a pollen grain on a stigma

The female gametes are inside the **ovules**, inside the **ovaries**. Each ovule contains a structure called an **embryo sac**. This contains six haploid cells and one diploid cell.

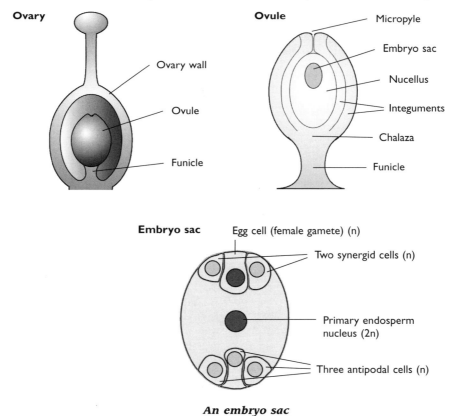

An embryo sac

The pollen tube grows down through the style and enters the ovule through a little gap in its coverings called the **micropyle**. Once the tube has reached the embryo sac, the tube nucleus disintegrates. The two male gametes enter the embryo sac. One of them fuses with the egg cell, forming a diploid zygote. The other fuses with the diploid nucleus, forming a triploid **endosperm nucleus**. (A triploid cell has three complete sets of chromosomes.)

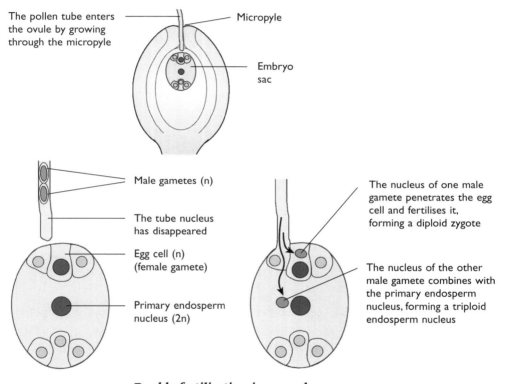

The pollen tube enters the ovule by growing through the micropyle

Micropyle

Embryo sac

Male gametes (n)

The tube nucleus has disappeared

Egg cell (n) (female gamete)

Primary endosperm nucleus (2n)

The nucleus of one male gamete penetrates the egg cell and fertilises it, forming a diploid zygote

The nucleus of the other male gamete combines with the primary endosperm nucleus, forming a triploid endosperm nucleus

Double fertilisation in an embryo sac

This strange double fertilisation is found only in flowering plants. The diploid zygote will develop into the embryo, eventually growing into a new plant. The triploid endosperm nucleus will divide to form a tissue called the **endosperm**, which provides nutrients for the young embryo during its early stages of germination. The whole ovule becomes a **seed**.

Importance of fertilisation in sexual reproduction

By definition, sexual reproduction involves fertilisation. Fertilisation is defined as the fusion of the nuclei of two gametes. Female gametes will generally not develop until they have been fertilised.

Two haploid gametes fuse to produce a diploid zygote. Fertilisation produces a zygote with one set of chromosomes from each of two different parents. This increases genetic variability among the offspring.

Stem cells

In a multicellular organ, most cells are specialised for a particular function. Some cells, however, remain unspecialised. They are called **stem cells** and they retain the ability to divide and produce daughter cells which can become specialised for particular functions.

Soon after fertilisation, a zygote divides repeatedly to form numerous cells making up an embryo. These early cells are all stem cells, often known as **embryonic stem cells**. They are able to produce new cells that can develop into any of the specialised cell types present in an adult body. They are therefore known as **totipotent** stem cells.

As the embryo develops, fewer and fewer totipotent stem cells remain. Many, however, retain the ability to divide to make many (but not all) different types of cells, and these are called **pluripotent** stem cells.

Making use of stem cells

It is hoped that stem cells can be used to cure many human diseases. For example, Parkinson's disease is caused by the loss of neurones in the brain that are able to produce a neurotransmitter called dopamine. If stem cells could be introduced into the brain and stimulated to divide to make new dopamine-producing neurones, this would relieve the symptoms of the disease.

It is not easy, however, to find suitable sources of stem cells. Most stem cells in an adult human are only able to divide to produce a very few types of specialised cells. For example, stem cells in the bone marrow can produce red and white blood cells. They cannot produce heart muscle or neurones.

Embryonic stem cells are especially useful because they are totipotent or pluripotent. It is possible to remove a cell from a very young human embryo produced by *in vitro* fertilisation without harming the development of the embryo. However, there are ethical issues associated with the use of embryonic stem cells. Some people consider that it is not acceptable to use embryos for this purpose.

Even if embryonic stem cells could be harvested and used, they will not be readily accepted into the body of another person, as the immune system will recognise that they are foreign and will attempt to destroy them. It would therefore be better if we could use stem cells obtained from a person's own body.

It may become possible to take 'ordinary' cells, such as skin cells, and reprogram them to become stem cells.

Tissue culture

Plants also contain stem cells. You can use these to grow a complete new plant. There are many different methods for doing this, but an especially good one involves growing complete cauliflower plants from a small piece of a floret (the white part that you eat). The florets contain totipotent stem cells. A complete set of instructions for doing this can be found at www-saps.plantsci.cam.ac.uk/prac_tech.htm. Click on the link to the cauliflower tissue culture method.

All equipment and materials that you use must be sterilised, either with disinfectant or by heating to high temperatures. You also need to sterilise the cauliflower florets, by immersing them in sodium hypochlorite solution for 10 minutes. They should then be rinsed in sterile water.

Cut each floret into tiny pieces no larger than 5 mm². These are called explants. Each explant should be placed into sterile growing medium in a sterile container, and incubated. The explants will grow into embryo plants, which can then be grown on to produce adult plants.

Tissue culture is used commercially to produce large numbers of genetically identical plants. It is especially useful where it is difficult to propagate the plants in any other way, for example for propagating orchids.

How cells become specialised

Each cell in a multicellular organism — such as a human or a cauliflower plant — has been produced by mitosis from the original zygote or stem cells. All of its cells are therefore genetically identical. Each cell contains two complete sets of chromosomes, each with a complete set of genes.

When a cell specialises to carry out a particular function, the genes that it will need are switched on, and all of those it does not need are switched off. For example, a muscle cell will have the genes for making actin and myosin (proteins essential for muscle contraction) switched on, but the gene for making keratin (the protein in hair) will be switched off.

The genes in the 'switched on' set are transcribed, producing mRNA. The mRNA is used to guide protein synthesis, by determining the sequence in which amino acids are linked together on a ribosome. Many of the proteins that are made are enzymes, and these will catalyse a particular set of metabolic reactions, thereby determining the functions of the cell. Other proteins are structural — for example actin and myosin in a muscle cell.

The process in which a 'generalist' cell becomes a specialised cell is known as **differentiation**. Stem cells are undifferentiated cells.

Phenotype

The phenotype of a cell is its observable or measurable features. We have seen in Unit 1 how genes affect phenotype. Frequently, environment also affects phenotype.

Hair colour in cats

Many different genes determine hair colour in cats. At least eight different genes, at different loci, are known to influence hair colour and it is thought that there are probably more. These are known as **polygenes**. Depending on the particular combination of alleles that a cat has for each of these genes, it can have any of a very wide range of colours. Hair colour in cats is an example of **continuous variation**. This is variation in which there are no clear-cut categories. There is a continuous range of variation in colour between the lightest and darkest extremes.

The cat hair colour genes exert their effect by coding for the production of enzymes. One such gene is found at the C locus. Siamese cats have two copies of a recessive allele of this gene called c^s. This gene codes for an enzyme which is sensitive to temperature. It produces dark hair at the extremities of paws, ears and tail where the temperature is lower, and light hair in warmer parts of the body. The colouring of a Siamese cat is therefore the result of interaction between genes and environment.

The hair is darker in areas which are colder, such as the ears and paws

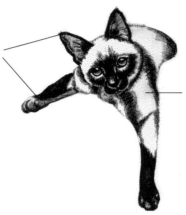

The hair is lighter in areas which are warmer, such as the body

Hair colour in a Siamese cat

Human height

Human height is also affected by many different genes at different loci. It is also affected by environment. Even if a person inherits alleles of these genes that give the potential to grow tall, he or she will not grow tall unless the diet supplies plenty of nutrients to allow this to happen. Poor nutrition, especially in childhood, reduces the maximum height that is attained.

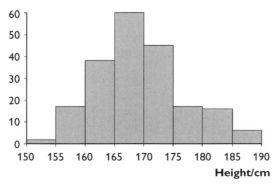

This histogram shows that the heights of a group of people have a normal distribution

Continuous variation is generally the result of polygenes, or of interaction between genes and the environment

Continuous variation in human height

Cancer

The risk of developing cancer is influenced by both genes and environment. For example, a woman with the alleles *BRCA1* or *BRCA2* has a 50–80% of chance of developing breast cancer at some stage in her life. This is a much higher risk than for people who do not have these alleles. The normal alleles of these genes protect cells from changes that could lead to them becoming cancerous.

However, environment also affects this risk. Smoking, for example, increases the risk even further. Taking the drug tamoxifen can reduce the risk.

Monoamine oxidase A

Monoamine oxidase A (MAO-A) is an enzyme that is found associated with mitochondria in the nervous system, and also in the liver and digestive system. In the nervous system, it is involved in the inactivation of neurotransmitters including noradrenaline and serotonin.

Some alleles of the monoamine oxidase gene produce low-activity MAO-A, while others produce high-activity MAO-A. It has been found that children with the high-activity form, if maltreated, are more likely to show antisocial behaviour than similarly treated children with the low-activity form.

Other behaviours, such as novelty seeking, also appear to be associated with particular alleles of this gene. However, in all cases the environment also has large effects on behaviour; behaviour is produced by interaction between this gene (and probably others as yet unidentified) and the environment.

Interpreting the data

It is difficult to interpret data to decide just how much effect the MAO-A gene is having, because:

- the environments of the subjects are likely to be very different from each other, so however hard the researchers try to control other variables they may be unable to do so effectively
- the contribution of the gene is often very small, compared with the effect of the environment
- there may be many other genes that are also having an effect on the characteristic being studied
- numbers in studies are usually fairly small, so it is not easy to obtain statistically reliable results
- the characteristic being studied may not be easy to define

Biodiversity and natural resources

Structure and function of plant tissues

Plant cells

Plant cells are eukaryotic cells. They are very similar in structure to animal cells, containing all the structures shown in the diagram on page 13 except centrioles. Plant cells also contain structures not present in animal cells. These include:

- **chloroplasts** — organelles surrounded by an envelope (two membranes) and containing chlorophyll, in which photosynthesis takes place
- **amyloplasts** — organelles surrounded by an envelope, in which starch is stored
- **vacuole** — a space bounded by a membrane known as the **tonoplast**, containing cell sap

Plant cells have a **cell wall** on the outside of the cell membrane. The cell wall is made of cellulose fibres embedded in a matrix of **calcium pectate** and other substances. The cell walls of adjacent plant cells are generally held together by a middle lamella.

Adjacent plant cells are often connected by **plasmodesmata** (singular: plasmodesma). These are little gaps in the cell walls through which the cell surface membranes of the two cells connect. They form channels through which substances can easily pass from the cytoplasm or one cell to the other, without having to pass through a membrane.

There may also be **pits** in the cell wall, where the cell wall is thinner and it is easier for substances to diffuse across it.

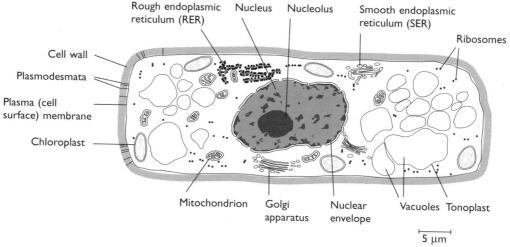

Ultrastructure of a plant cell

Starch and cellulose

Both starch and cellulose are polysaccharides. They are polymers of glucose. Both consist of hundreds of glucose molecules linked together in long chains by glycosidic bonds.

Starch is an energy storage compound, found in many plant organs inside amyloplasts and chloroplasts. It can be hydrolysed to glucose and respired when energy is required.

Cellulose is a structural compound, which forms the fibres of which plant cell walls are made. It is difficult to hydrolyse, as there are few enzymes that can break the links between the glucose molecules in the chain.

These different functions are related to the different molecular structures of starch and cellulose.

- In starch, the glucose molecules are α-glucose, and the links between the molecules are **α 1–4 glycosidic bonds**. In cellulose, the glucose molecules are β-glucose, and the links are **β 1–4 glycosidic bonds**.
- The α 1–4 links in starch (amylose) cause the chain to curl into a spiral. The β 1–4 links in cellulose cause the chain to remain straight.
- Hydrogen bonds form between different glucose units in a starch molecule, holding the molecule in a spiral shape. This makes it compact and good for storage. In cellulose, hydrogen bonds form between different molecules, holding many molecules together in parallel, forming bundles called **microfibrils**. These have high tensile strength.

α-glucose and β-glucose

Starch contains chains of α1–4 linked glucose

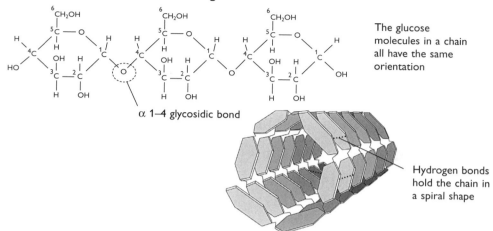

The glucose molecules in a chain all have the same orientation

α 1–4 glycosidic bond

Hydrogen bonds hold the chain in a spiral shape

Cellulose contains chains of β1–4 linked glucose

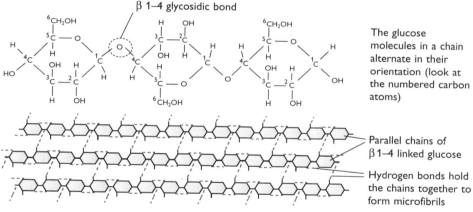

β 1–4 glycosidic bond

The glucose molecules in a chain alternate in their orientation (look at the numbered carbon atoms)

Parallel chains of β1–4 linked glucose

Hydrogen bonds hold the chains together to form microfibrils

Molecular structure of starch and cellulose

The plant cell wall

A plant cell wall is made of cellulose microfibrils embedded in a matrix of pectin and other compounds.

The cell wall is laid down at the surface of the cell. As new layers are laid down, the older ones are pushed further away from the cell surface membrane.

The first part of the cell wall to be laid down is called the **primary cell wall**. It is fairly thin, and has cellulose microfibrils running in all directions. Later, the **secondary cell wall** is laid down. This is much thicker and has several layers, each with cellulose microfibrils running parallel to each other, but in different directions in each layer. This provides a very strong structure, resistant to tearing. The cell wall helps to prevent a plant cell from bursting when it has taken up water and is turgid.

In between the cell walls of adjacent plant cells there is a **middle lamella**. This is made of calcium pectate, which holds the cells firmly together.

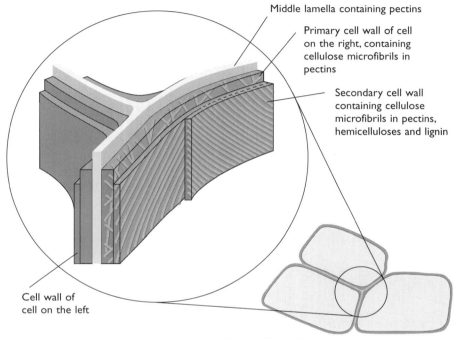

Middle lamella containing pectins

Primary cell wall of cell on the right, containing cellulose microfibrils in pectins

Secondary cell wall containing cellulose microfibrils in pectins, hemicelluloses and lignin

Cell wall of cell on the left

Structure of plant cell walls

Making use of cellulose
The cellulose microfibrils from cotton bolls (the seed heads of cotton plants) are used to make cotton fibres. The strands of cellulose are spun together to make thread, which is then woven to produce cloth.

Specialised plant cells
Plants contain many different types of cells that have become specialised to carry out particular functions. Two of these are sclerenchyma fibres and xylem vessels.

Sclerenchyma fibres are long, thin cells whose cell walls have filled up with **lignin**. Lignin is a very hard, strong substance — wood is made of lignin. It is waterproof, so once it has impregnated a cell wall, water can no longer pass through it and the cell contents die. Sclerenchyma fibres help to support plant stems.

Xylem vessels are long tubes through which water is transported from the roots of a plant to all other regions. They have lignin in their cell walls, and no living contents. Their end walls usually break down completely, so that many xylem vessels stacked end to end form a continuous tube. There are pits in their walls allowing water to move sideways from one vessel to a neighbouring one, or into the surrounding tissues. As well as transporting water, they transport mineral salts in solution. They are also important in providing support.

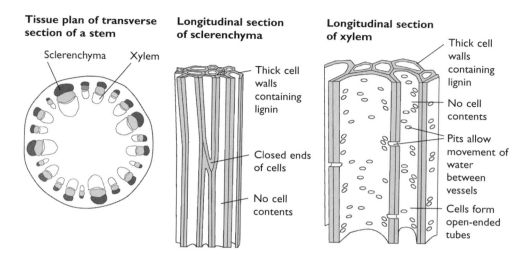

Sclerenchyma and xylem vessels in a plant stem

Making use of plant fibres and starch

Sclerenchyma fibres and xylem vessels from plant stems or leaves can be used to make fibres for human use. For example, flax fibres are obtained from the stems of flax plants, and can be woven to produce linen. Sisal is obtained from the leaves of agave plants.

The starch stores in plants provide important food for people all over the world. Starch stores in cereal grains are especially important; maize, rice and wheat are staple foods in many countries. Potatoes, which are underground stem tubers, also contain large amounts of starch.

Starch can also be used as a food for microorganisms, which can metabolise the starch to produce substances for uses other than food. For example, starch from maize grains can be broken down to produce sugars, which can then be fermented by yeast to produce alcohol. This can be used to make **biofuels**.

Starch can also be used to make **plastics**. This can be done, for example, by treating starch with solvents and blending it with other materials. Many of these plastics are biodegradable, so they cause fewer disposal problems than other types of plastics. Plastics are normally made from oil or other fossil fuels, and most of them are not biodegradable.

Using starch to make biofuels and plastics can decrease our use of fossil fuels, and so may contribute to **sustainability**. However, large areas of land are required to grow the crops to produce the starch. This can mean that less land is used to grow food, so food prices may increase. It can also cause areas of natural forest to be cleared in order to grow more crops.

Determining the tensile strength of plant fibres

Tensile strength is the ability of a material to withstand pulling forces.

You can use plant fibres taken from a fabric (for example linen or cotton), or from a plant (for example vascular bundles stripped from a celery petiole or 'hairs' from a coconut).

Fix one end of the fibre very firmly to a support such as a clamp on a retort stand.

Tie the other end of the fibre to a loop made of a light-weight material that you know is stronger than the plant fibre (for example extra-strong polyester thread).

Hang a small mass from the loop. The downward force in newtons exerted by the mass is calculated by multiplying the mass in kilograms by 10.

Continue to add masses until the fibre breaks.

You can also:

- measure the extension of the plant fibre as you apply a force to it, and plot extension against load. To do this, you can fix a ruler graduated in mm behind the plant fibre. The extension of the fibre is its new length minus its original length.
- compare the tensile strength of different fibres. You will need to use fibres of approximately the same diameter.
- compare the tensile strength of a single fibre with that of a number of fibres arranged parallel to one another, or a number of fibres twisted around one another.

Water and inorganic ions in plants

Plants absorb water and inorganic ions from the soil, into their root hairs. The water and ions move across the root towards its centre. They enter the xylem vessels and are transported through the xylem to all other parts of the plant.

Plants need water for:

- **photosynthesis.** Water is combined with carbon dioxide in chloroplasts to produce glucose. Oxygen is produced as a waste product.
- maintaining **turgor.** Soft tissues of plants are held in shape by the turgor of their cells. Cells absorb water by osmosis through their cell surface membranes, whenever the water potential outside the cell is greater than inside. A cell that holds plenty of water swells and pushes outwards on its cell wall, and is said to be turgid. A tissue made of turgid cells is firm and well supported.
- **transport.** Many substances are transported in aqueous solution. Inorganic ions such as magnesium and nitrate are transported in solution in xylem vessels. Sucrose and amino acids are transported in solution in phloem sieve tubes.
- **cooling.** Water continuously evaporates from the wet cell walls of spongy mesophyll cells, diffusing into the air spaces in the leaf. This evaporation takes heat from the cell walls, helping to cool the plant. The water vapour then diffuses out of the leaf through the stomata, a process known as transpiration.

Plants need many different inorganic ions. The ions are usually absorbed by active transport into the root hairs. They include:

- **nitrate.** Nitrate ions are used to convert carbohydrates (made in photosynthesis) to amino acids and nucleotides. The amino acids are then used to make proteins, many of which act as enzymes. Nucleotides are used to make RNA and DNA.
- **calcium ions.** The matrix of the cell wall, and the middle lamella, are made of calcium pectate. Calcium ions are also used in signalling. For example, exposure to stress such as drought or extreme temperatures may cause a cell to take up calcium ions, which causes a particular set of genes to be switched on. Calcium ions are essential in the formation of microtubules, and therefore cell division.
- **magnesium.** Chlorophyll molecules contain magnesium. Each chlorophyll molecule contains a porphyrin ring with a central magnesium ion. Magnesium ions are also essential for the activity of many enzymes, including those involved with glycolysis and the Calvin cycle.

Investigating the effect of mineral deficiency on plant growth

You can find out how the lack of a particular inorganic ion (mineral) affects plant growth using culture solutions. Some plants can be grown in a culture solution containing all the ions you are investigating. Others are grown in solutions which each lack just one of the ions.

The easiest way to obtain the different solutions is to buy them as a kit from an educational supplier. It is also possible to make up your own solutions.

The plants you use should be young seedlings. You could try different species to compare the effects of a particular deficiency on each one. Cereal seedlings (for example wheat) or other small plants (such as radishes) work well.

The seedlings should be grown in identical conditions and be the same age. They should then be washed thoroughly with sterile distilled water before you place their roots in the culture solution. All equipment and materials must be sterilised before use. If the solution and roots are in a transparent container, it must be covered with black paper or foil to prevent light entering. You may need to bubble air through the medium to ensure that the roots have sufficient oxygen to take up the minerals by active transport.

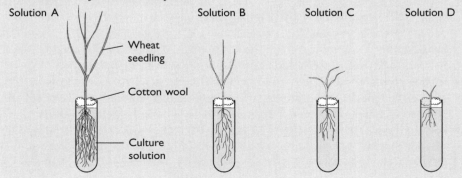

Solution A — Wheat seedling — Cotton wool — Culture solution

Solution B

Solution C

Solution D

content guidance

Investigating the antimicrobial properties of plants

Many plants produce compounds that inhibit the growth of microorganisms. Plants with strong scents or tastes that we use in food preparation (such as garlic, herbs, mustard) are especially likely to have antimicrobial properties.

First, obtain a sterile Petri dish containing sterile nutrient agar jelly. Using sterile technique, flood the surface of the agar with a small amount of nutrient broth containing a culture of harmless bacteria.

Make up some samples of plant material to test. One way of doing this is to crush a small amount of the plant tissue using a pestle and mortar, and then add a small amount of sterile water to it.

Using a sterile cork borer, cut out several small holes in the surface of the agar jelly. Mark the base of the Petri dish with labels for each well. Use sterile pipettes to introduce a few drops of sterile water to one well as a control, and a different plant material to each of the other wells. Cover and incubate.

The bacteria will reproduce and form visible colonies on the surface of the agar. Substances from the plant material will diffuse out of the well into the agar. If clear areas — that is bacteria-free areas — are visible around a particular well, this indicates that the substance in the well inhibits bacterial growth.

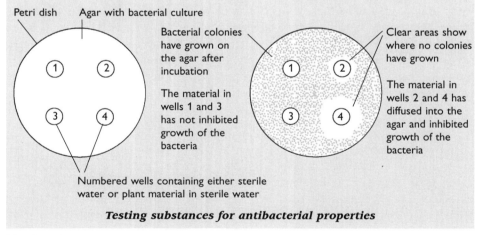

Testing substances for antibacterial properties

Testing drugs

Many medicinal drugs are derived from substances first found in plants. For example, the drug digitalin was discovered in the foxglove, *Digitalis*. Extracts from foxgloves, usually mixed with many other plant substances, were used as folk remedies for dropsy (which we now know as congestive heart failure) for hundreds of years. In 1775 an English doctor, William Withering, determined that the active ingredient of this herbal preparation was the substance that came from foxgloves. He tried out different methods of preparation and dosages on 156 patients, and then published his recommendations to help other doctors to prescribe the drug appropriately.

Today, trials of new drugs are much more rigorous. First, the drug is tried out in the laboratory, to determine its effects on living cells or on animals. It then undergoes a three-phase trial before it can be marketed.

Phase I involves giving the drug to a small number of healthy volunteers under very carefully controlled conditions. The purpose of this phase is to check for any harmful side effects of the drug, and to collect information about what is a safe dosage. The drug only goes on to Phase II if it passes this test.

Phase II involves about 200–400 people, including some who have the condition that the drug is intended to treat. The group will ideally contain both men and women of a wide age range. The purpose of this phase is to determine whether the drug does help to treat the condition, what is the most effective dosage, how it compares with other treatments already in existence, and the severity of any side effects. The volunteers are closely monitored throughout the trial.

Phase III is reached only by relatively few drugs, as most do not pass Phases I and II. In Phase III, the drug is tested on several thousand patients. This time, the drug is used as it is intended it will be once it is marketed, with the volunteers going about their own lives in a normal way. This will find out if people are able to take it, and remember to take it, in the recommended manner and how well it works in 'normal' conditions.

If the drug passes all of these trials, it can be marketed. Even after it is marketed, **Phase IV** testing is carried out, in which information is collected about the effects of the drug. Sometimes, side effects come to light in this phase that were not noted previously, because now the drug is being used by much larger numbers of people. If this happens, and the side effects are sufficiently serious, the drug may have to be withdrawn.

Placebos and double blind trials

A **placebo** is a treatment that does not contain any active ingredient. It is known that people often respond to a placebo in a similar way to a drug (so long as they do not know it is a placebo). For example, if a patient is given a pill or injection and told it contains an active drug, their symptoms may be relieved in a similar way to that expected to result from drug treatment. It is therefore important that, when testing the effectiveness of a drug, it is compared with a placebo. To be useful, a drug must have a significantly greater effect than a placebo.

The results of a trial are only valid if the patient, the person giving the 'drug' and those recording the results do not know whether the patient was given the real drug or just a placebo. These people are therefore all kept in the dark about which patients are receiving the drug or a placebo. This is known as a **double blind trial**.

Biodiversity

Biodiversity can be defined as the range of habitats, communities and species in an area, and the genetic variation that exists within the populations of each species. (A **community** can be defined as all the different organisms, of all the different species, that live in the same place at the same time.)

Measuring biodiversity

We can find out something about the biodiversity of an area by measuring the **species richness**. This is the number of different species in the area. The greater the species richness, the greater the biodiversity.

We can also investigate the number of different alleles in the gene pool of the species. This is a measure of **genetic diversity**. The gene pool is all the different alleles, of all the different genes, in a population. A **population** can be defined as all the individuals of a particular species that live in the same place at the same time.

It is not possible to discover and count every single allele in a population. Sometimes, researchers may simply record the range of different features in the population, such as the range of hair colour. More usefully, they may collect DNA samples and analyse the base sequences to look for variations between individuals. The more variation in base sequences, the greater the genetic diversity.

It is generally considered desirable for a species to have reasonably large genetic diversity. This means that if the environment changes — for example, because of climate change or if a new pathogen emerges — then at least some of the population may possess features that will enable them to survive. Genetic diversity allows species to become adapted to a changing environment.

Endemism

Some species are only found in one country or one small area. They are said to be **endemic** to that area. This may happen if a habitat has been isolated from others for a long time, so that the species in the habitat have evolved quite separately from those elsewhere. For example, Madagascar — a large island in the Indian Ocean off the coast of southern Africa — has been isolated from all other land for about 80 million years. This explains why a very high proportion of the animals and plant species in Madagascar are endemic.

Adaptation to the environment

Organisms do not live in isolation from each other or from their environment. Living organisms constantly interact with their environment. The interactions between living organisms and each other, and between the organisms and their non-living environment (for example, the soil, air, rocks and water) are known as an **ecosystem**.

The individual members of every species must be able to survive and reproduce in their environment, if the species is to continue to exist. Each species can be said to have its own **niche** in an ecosystem. The niche is sometimes said to be the 'role' of the organism. It includes the ways in which it interacts with other organisms — for example, what it eats and what eats it — and also the ways in which it interacts with its environment — for example, the level of humidity it requires for survival, or the kind of nesting site it needs.

The niches of different species are never completely identical. Two species with very similar niches are likely to **compete** with each other. Competition results when two individuals both require the same resource which is in short supply. Generally, species with greatly overlapping niches will not coexist. One will always outcompete the other.

Each individual member of the species has features that allow it to be successful in its environment, and to occupy its niche. These are known as **adaptations**. They may be behavioural, physiological or anatomical. ('Physiological' is to do with the way the body works, while 'anatomical' is to do with its structure.) The table shows a few examples.

Some examples of adaptations

Organism	Behavioural adaptation	Physiological adaptation	Anatomical adaptation
Earthworm	Responds extremely rapidly to a bird peck on its head by retracting into its burrow. Generally only comes out to feed at night.	Has blood containing haemoglobin which absorbs oxygen even in the relatively low oxygen concentrations underground.	Has stiff hairs called chaetae along its lower surface, which grip firmly onto the sides of its burrow and help it to move underground.
Venus fly trap	Leaves fold when sensitive hairs are touched.	Cells in leaf surface secrete hydrolytic enzymes that digest trapped insects.	Leaves have a fringe of stiff hairs that prevents insects escaping when the leaf has folded.
Salmon	When adult, leaves the sea and swims upstream along the river in which it was born, to find a place to spawn.	Gills are able to switch from excreting salt when in the sea to taking it up by active transport when in fresh water.	Adult fish have unusually strong swimming muscles that allow them to swim upstream in fast-flowing rivers and even to leap up waterfalls.

Natural selection

Adaptations evolve through natural selection. In a population, not every organism will have exactly the same alleles or exactly the same features. There will be genetic variation within the population. Those organisms whose particular set of features are best suited to the environment are most likely to survive. Those with less useful features are more likely to die.

The organisms with the most useful features are therefore more likely to reach adulthood and reproduce. Their alleles will be passed on to their offspring. Over many generations, the alleles that confer useful characteristics on an individual are therefore likely to become more common. Alleles that do not produce such useful characteristics are less likely to be passed on to successive generations and will become less common.

This process is called **natural selection**. Over time, it ensures that the individuals in a population have features that enable them to survive and reproduce in their environment.

Stabilising and directional selection

When the environment is fairly stable, natural selection is unlikely to bring about change. If the organisms in a population are already well adapted to their environment, then the most common alleles in the population will be those that confer an advantage on the organisms, and it is these alleles that continue to be passed on to successive generations. This is called **stabilising selection**.

However, if the environment changes, alleles that were previously advantageous may become disadvantageous. For example, the individuals in a species of mammal may have white fur which camouflages them against the snow and confers an advantage in escaping predators. If the climate changes so that snow no longer lies on the ground, then animals with white fur may be more likely to be killed by predators than animals with brown fur. Those with brown fur are now most likely to reproduce and pass on their alleles to the next generation. Over time, brown may become the most common fur colour in the population. This is an example of **directional selection**.

Stabilising selection

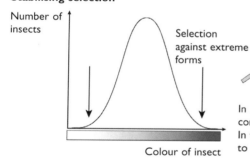

Number of insects

Selection against extreme forms

Colour of insect

In stabilising selection the forms at the extremes of a continuous variation are at a selective disadvantage. In this case, very light and very dark insects are easier to see on the leaf and more likely to be eaten by birds.

Directional selection

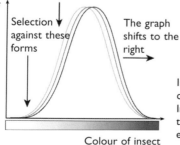

Number of insects

Selection against these forms

The graph shifts to the right

Colour of insect

In directional selection, one of the extreme forms of a continuous variation are at a selective advantage. In this case, dark insects are harder to see on the leaf than light insects, so dark insects are less likely to be eaten by birds.

Stabilising and directional selection

Directional selection may result in **evolution**. Evolution can be defined as a long-term change in the characteristics of a species. Eventually, the changes may become so great that the new population is unable to breed with members of the original species. A new species has therefore been produced.

Classification

Biologists classify organisms according to how closely they believe they are related to one another. Each species has evolved from a previously existing species. We do not usually have any information about these ancestral species, so we judge the degree of relatedness between two organisms by looking carefully at their physiology, anatomy and biochemistry. The greater the similarities, the more closely they are thought to be related.

The system used for classification is a **taxonomic system**. This involves placing organisms in a series of taxonomic units which form a hierarchy. The largest unit is the **kingdom**. Kingdoms are subdivided into phyla, classes, orders, families, genera and species.

An example of classification

Kingdom	Animalia
Phylum	Chordates
Class	Mammalia
Order	Rodentia
Family	Muridae
Genus	*Mus*
Species	*Mus musculus* (house mouse)

Five kingdoms and three domains

Until quite recently, biologists classified all living organisms into five kingdoms. These are:

- **Kingdom Prokaryota** — these are organisms with prokaryotic cells (page 13). This kingdom includes bacteria and blue-green algae.
- **Kingdom Protoctista** — these organisms have eukaryotic cells. They mostly exist as single cells, but some are made of groups of similar cells.
- **Kingdom Fungi** — fungi have eukaryotic cells surrounded by a cell wall, but this is not made of cellulose, and fungi never have chloroplasts.
- **Kingdom Plantae** — these are the plants. They have eukaryotic cells surrounded by cellulose cell walls and they feed by photosynthesis.
- **Kingdom Animalia** — these are the animals. They have eukaryotic cells with no cell wall.

However, in 1990 new information led to the proposal of a completely new classification. This resulted from new discoveries about the metabolic pathways (sequences of chemical reactions) taking place in prokaryotic organisms. Although all prokaryotic organisms have structural similarities, it was discovered that they can have very different molecular biology and biochemistry. These include:

- differences in the structure of their cell membranes and cell walls
- differences in the structure of their flagella (whip-like extensions that can move the cell through water)
- differences in the way in which information in DNA is used to build proteins.

As a result of this new information, the prokaryotes are now classified as two **domains**, the **Archaea** and the **Bacteria**. They are thought to be as widely different from each other as humans are from bacteria. All other organisms are classified as **Eukarya**.

Five kingdoms

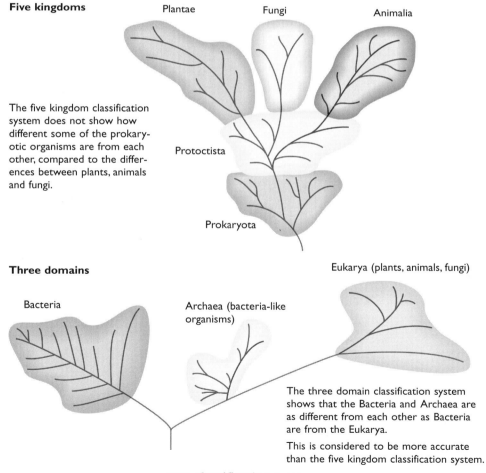

The five kingdom classification system does not show how different some of the prokaryotic organisms are from each other, compared to the differences between plants, animals and fungi.

Three domains

The three domain classification system shows that the Bacteria and Archaea are as different from each other as Bacteria are from the Eukarya.

This is considered to be more accurate than the five kingdom classification system.

Two classification systems

Zoos and seed banks in conservation

Conservation aims to maintain biodiversity. Increasing human populations exert pressure on other species, especially through habitat loss and pollution. Many species are under threat of extinction. The best way to conserve threatened species is in their own natural habitat, but this is not always possible. Zoos and seed banks have roles to play in helping conservation of organisms that cannot be conserved in their habitat.

Zoos can help through:

- **captive breeding programmes** — this involves collecting together a small group of organisms of a threatened species and encouraging them to breed together. In this way, extinction can be prevented. The breeding programme will try to maintain or even increase genetic diversity in the population by breeding unrelated animals together. This can be done by moving males from one zoo to another, or by using *in vitro* fertilisation with frozen sperm transported from males in another zoo. It may also be possible to implant embryos into a surrogate mother of a different species, so that many young can be produced even though there is only a small number of females of the endangered species.
- **reintroduction programmes** — the best captive breeding programmes work towards reintroducing individuals to their original habitats, if this can be made safe for them. It is important that work is done on the ground to prepare the habitat for the eventual reintroduction of the animals. For example, the scimitar-horned oryx has been successfully reintroduced to Tunisia, following a widespread captive breeding programme in European zoos and the preparation and protection of suitable habitat, including education and involvement of people living in or around the proposed reintroduction area.
- **education** — zoos can bring conservation issues to the attention of large numbers of people, who may decide to contribute financially towards conservation efforts or to campaign for them. Entrance fees and donations can be used to fund conservation programmes both in the zoo itself and in natural habitats.
- **research** — animals in zoos can be studied to find out more about their needs in terms of food, breeding places and so on. This can help to inform people working on conservation in natural habitats.

Seed banks store seeds collected from plants. Many seeds will live for a long time in cool, dry conditions, but others need more specialised storage environments. A few of the seeds are germinated every so often so that fresh seed can be collected and stored.

Seed banks can help conservation of plants just as zoos can help conservation of animals. The Royal Botanic Gardens, Kew, has a huge seed bank at Wakehurst Place, Sussex. Collectors search for seeds, especially those of rare or threatened species, and bring them to the seed bank where they are carefully stored. Another seed bank, built into the permafrost (permanently frozen ground) in Norway, aims to preserve seeds from all the world's food crops.

Questions
&
Answers

In this section there are two sample examination papers, similar to the Edexcel Unit Test papers. All of the questions are based on the topic areas described in the previous sections of the book.

You have 1 hour 15 minutes to do each paper. There are 80 marks on the paper, so you can spend almost 1 minute per mark. If you find you are spending too long on one question, move on to another that you can answer more quickly. If you have time at the end, come back to the difficult one.

Some of the questions require you to recall information that you have learned. Be guided by the number of marks awarded to suggest how much detail you should give in your answer. The more marks there are, the more information you need to give.

Some of the questions require you to use your knowledge and understanding in new situations. Don't be surprised to find something completely new in a question — something you have not seen before. Just think carefully about it, and find something that you *do* know that will help you to answer it.

Do think carefully before you begin to write. The best answers are short and relevant — if you target your answer well, you can get a lot of marks for a small amount of writing. Don't ramble on and say the same thing several times over, or wander off into answers that have nothing to do with the question. As a general rule, there will be twice as many answer lines as marks. So you should try to answer a 3 mark question in no more than 6 lines of writing. If you are writing much more than that, you almost certainly haven't focused your answer tightly enough.

Look carefully at exactly what each question wants you to do. For example, if it asks you to 'Explain', you need to say *how* or *why* something happens, not just *what* happens. Many students lose large numbers of marks by not reading the question carefully.

Following each question, there is an answer that might get a C or D grade, followed by an examiner's comments, indicated by 🄔. Then there is an answer that might get an A or B grade, again followed by examiner's comments. You might like to try answering the questions yourself first, before looking at these.

Question 1

The diagram below shows part of the small intestine of a mouse. The inner wall of the small intestine is made up of many tiny folds called villi. Between the villi are indentations known as crypts of Lieberkühn. The cells on the villus surface are specialised for the production of digestive enzymes and the absorption of the products of digestion.

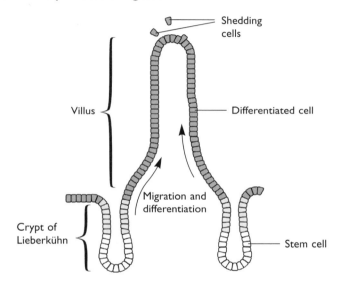

Cells at the upper surfaces of the villi are constantly shed. They are replaced by new cells which are produced from stem cells in the crypts and steadily work their way upwards. As they move upwards they differentiate.

(a) Give the term for a group of similar cells such as those covering the surface of a villus. (1 mark)

(b) Explain what is meant by the term *stem cell*. (2 marks)

(c) State whether or not the stem cells in the crypts of Lieberkühn are totipotent. Explain your answer. (2 marks)

(d) Suggest the changes that will take place in the cells as they differentiate. (4 marks)

(e) (i) Outline the reasons why embryonic stem cells may be useful in medical therapies. (4 marks)

(ii) **Suggest why some people may have ethical objections to the use of embryonic stem cells for such therapies.** (2 marks)

Total: 15 marks

■ ■ ■

Candidate A

(a) Tissue ✓

> 🖉 Correct. 1/1

(b) A cell that can divide ✓ and produce new cells.

> 🖉 Partly correct, but not enough for the second mark. 1/2

(c) No, because only embryonic stem cells are totipotent.

> 🖉 Although 'No' is correct, there is no mark for this; both marks are for the explanation. This is not a good answer, because it does not relate directly to the cells in the questions, nor does it explain what totipotent means. 0/2

(d) They will become able to produce digestive enzymes ✓ and will move up the villus.

> 🖉 Much more detail is expected than is given in this answer. The candidate has not described what will change in the cells as they differentiate. 1/4

(e) (i) They could be used to cure Alzheimer's or Parkinson's. ✓ You could put stem cells into the brain and they will make new cells that work properly.

> 🖉 The candidate gives two examples of diseases that could be treated with stem cells, but does not mention why embryonic stem cells would be especially useful, or how the stem cells might treat the disease. 1/4

(ii) To get the cells, you have to kill embryos. ✓

> 🖉 Once again, this answer does not have sufficient depth. 1/2

Candidate B

(a) Tissue ✓

> 🖉 Correct. 1/1

(b) It is a cell that has not differentiated ✓, and can keep on dividing to produce new cells ✓. These new cells can then differentiate into specialised cells.

> 🖉 A good answer. 2/2

(c) No. Totipotent stem cells are able to produce all the different kinds of specialised cells ✓. These stem cells only make cells for the surface of the villus ✓.

> 🖉 A very clear and entirely correct answer. The candidate has explained what 'totipotent' means, and then applied this knowledge to the particular stem cells in the question. 2/2

(d) Particular sets of genes would be switched on or off ✓. The cells would get more endoplasmic reticulum ✓ and Golgi apparatus ✓.

Again, a good answer with some very specific information. The candidate has only thought about enzyme synthesis, however, and not about the other function of the cells, which is absorption. The cells would also increase the number of mitochondria they contain (to provide energy for protein synthesis and active transport) and will develop microvilli (lots of small folds on their surfaces, to increase the surface area for absorption). 3/4

(e) (i) Some diseases, like Parkinson's ✓, are caused by certain groups of cells not working ✓. In Parkinson's disease, cells in the brain that should produce dopamine stop doing this ✓. If you could put stem cells into the brain then they might be able to divide and make new dopamine-producing cells ✓. This would mean the person might not need to keep taking drugs. Embryonic stem cells would be especially useful because they are able to form all the different kinds of cells ✓ in the body.

An excellent answer that gets the maximum marks available. 4/4

(ii) You have to kill embryos to get the cells. ✓

Correct as far as it goes, but more is needed for the second mark. For example, the candidate could have explained that the embryos will be ones that have been produced by *in vitro* fertilisation and that could otherwise be frozen and stored for later use. Another mark-worthy comment would be that people might want to produce embryos just so that they could get stem cells from them. 1/2

Question 2

(a) The diagram shows the mitotic cell cycle.

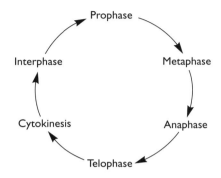

(i) On the diagram, write the letter **A** to indicate the stage at which
DNA replication occurs. (1 mark)

(ii) On the diagram, write the letter **B** to indicate the stage at which
the chromosomes line up on the equator of the spindle. (1 mark)

(b) Describe the events that occur during anaphase. (4 marks)

(c) A student made a root tip squash, stained it with acetic orcein and
observed it under a light microscope. She counted the number of cells
she could see in each stage of the cell cycle. The table shows her results.

Stage of cell cycle	Number of cells observed
Prophase	12
Metaphase	10
Anaphase	4
Telophase	6
Cytokinesis	8
Interphase	160

(i) Calculate the percentage of cells observed that were in
metaphase. Show your working. (2 marks)

(ii) Explain what these results show about the relative amount of time
the cells in this part of a plant spend in metaphase compared with
interphase. (2 marks)

(iii) Describe how the student would prepare the root tip squash, for
viewing under a light microscope. (4 marks)

Total: 14 marks

Candidate A

(a)

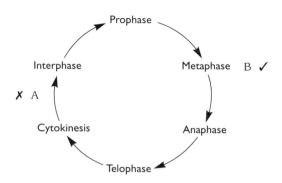

(i) Incorrect. The letter A needs to be clearly associated with interphase. 0/1

(ii) Correct. 1/1

(b) The chromosomes separate into chromatids. ✓ Each chromatid goes to the opposite end of the cell. ✓ Then new nuclear membranes form and the chromatids disappear.

The first two sentences are relevant and correct, but do not give enough information. The last sentence is about telophase, not anaphase. 2/4

(c) (i) 20 ✗

The answer is wrong and there is no working. 0/2

(ii) The cells must spend longer in metaphase than in anaphase, because there are more ✓ of them in metaphase at any one time. ✗

The candidate has misread the question, which was about *interphase* not anaphase. However, 1 mark can be awarded for the idea that if there are more cells in a particular stage, this means that stage lasts longer. 1/2

(iii) Get a root tip and put it on a microscope slide. Put some filter paper round it and squash it with a pencil. Put some red stain onto it and warm it over a Bunsen flame. ✓ Then look at it under a microscope.

It appears that the student has actually done this activity, as the description includes several steps that would be carried out. However, they are not in the correct sequence, there is quite a lot of essential detail missing and the stain is not named — perhaps the student had not noticed that it is actually mentioned in the question! 1/4

question 2

Candidate B

(a)

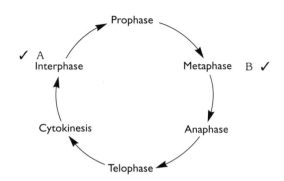

Prophase

✓ A
Interphase

Metaphase B ✓

Cytokinesis

Anaphase

Telophase

> 📝 (i) and (ii) Both correct. 2/2

(b) The spindle fibres, which are attached to the centromeres, pull ✓ them apart. ✓ As the spindle fibres shorten ✓, they pull the chromatids ✓ to opposite ends ✓ of the cell.

> 📝 An excellent answer. The candidate has mentioned that the centromeres split and the chromatids are separated and explains how the spindle fibres are involved in this process. Maximum 4/4

(c) (i) Total number of cells counted = 200

So percentage of cells in metaphase = $10/200 \times 100$ ✓= 5% ✓

> 📝 Working and answer are correct. 2/2

(ii) There are 10 cells in metaphase and 160 in interphase, so interphase must last 16 times ✓ longer ✓ than metaphase.

> 📝 Entirely correct, and includes a calculation of how much longer interphase lasts. 2/2

(iii) Cut off a root tip. Put it on a slide and add some acetic orcein. ✓ Hold the slide in your hand and warm it ✓ over a Bunsen flame. Put some more stain on it and cover it with a coverslip ✓. Wrap it in paper and tap with the blunt end of a pencil ✓ to squash the cells. Look at it under the microscope.

> 📝 This gets the maximum 4 marks, even though some detail is missing — for example, how much of the root tip to use and adding acid with the stain to help to break the cells apart. 4/4

Question 3

(a) The diagram shows a molecule of amylose (starch) and a molecule of cellulose.

Starch

Cellulose

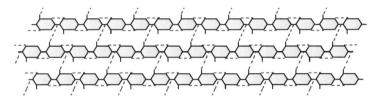

   (i)   **State *two* differences between the structure of an amylose molecule and the structure of a cellulose molecule.**   **(2 marks)**

   (ii) **Explain how these differences relate to the functions of these two molecules in a plant.**   **(8 marks)**

(b) **Outline the possible advantages of using starch-based products to replace plastics made from fossil fuels.**   **(3 marks)**

                                                                  Total: 13 marks

■ ■ ■

Candidate A

(a) (i) They are made of different sorts of glucose. They have different kinds of bonds holding the glucoses together.

     Both of these statements are correct, but they are not clear enough to get any marks. The candidate needs to say what the different kinds of glucose and bonds are, and which is found in which molecule. 0/2

   (ii) Starch molecules curl up in a spiral, which makes them compact ✓ and good for storage. Cellulose molecules make straight fibres, which makes them good for cell walls. ✓

     The candidate gets a mark for the idea that starch molecules are compact, and another mark for stating that starch is used for storage and cellulose for making cell walls. 2/8

(b) We don't have to use so many fossil fuels ✓, so it will reduce global warming.

🖉 This is a confused answer. It is true that, as most plastics are made from fossil fuels, using starch-based ones will reduce the use of these fuels — but as the fuels are not burnt and therefore do not release carbon dioxide in the process of making plastics this will have no effect on global warming. 1/3

Candidate B

(a) (i) Starch is made of alpha glucose and cellulose is made of beta glucose ✓. In starch the glucose units are all the same way up, but in cellulose they alternate ✓ one way and then the other way.

🖉 Two correct statements. 2/2

(ii) Starch is glucose molecules joined with alpha 1–4 glycosidic bonds. These are easy to break ✓ with amylase so the starch can be broken down to glucose and used in respiration to provide energy ✓. Because of the way up they are, the glucose molecules form hydrogen bonds with each other ✓ and make the chain twist into a helix ✓, so starch molecules pack a lot into a small space. This makes them good for storage ✓.

Cellulose is glucose molecules joined with beta 1–4 glycosidic bonds. These are difficult to break ✓ so cellulose is difficult for things to feed on so it makes a good protection ✓ round plant cells. The chains don't twist up like starch but stay straight ✓ and form hydrogen bonds with other chains ✓ making parallel groups of fibres ✓ which make cell walls strong.

🖉 An excellent answer. It clearly states what the functions of starch and cellulose are, and then makes clear links between their structures and these functions. Maximum 8/8

(b) Starch can be used to make plastics, instead of using oil. The plastics are biodegradable ✓ so there is not so much pollution.

🖉 The second sentence does not make clear that starch-based plastics are biodegradable whereas fossil-fuel based ones are not, but has rather generously been given the benefit of doubt. The candidate could also have stated that the use of starch-based plastics is more sustainable than using fossil fuels to make them, because fossil fuels are a finite resource and not renewable, whereas starch is produced from crops and is a renewable resource. 1/3

Question 4

Tigers, *Panthera tigris*, are a threatened species in the wild, largely due to loss of habitat and also hunting.

Tigers living in different parts of the world have measurable phenotypic differences from each other and have been assigned to different subspecies. For example, the Bengal tiger, *P. tigris tigris*, lives in India, while the Amur tiger, *P. tigris altaica*, lives in Siberia. Amur tigers tend to have thicker fur with paler golden stripes than Bengal tigers, and are heavier.

Zoos have been breeding tigers in captivity for over a century, and these captive tigers may be all that can save the species from exinction. For example, in 2008 there were 420 Amur tigers in captive breeding programmes, and about the same number living wild in Siberia. One subspecies, *P. tigris amoyensis*, the South China tiger, now exists only in captivity.

In the past, breeding programmes allowed tigers from different subspecies to breed with one another, but today care is taken that captive tigers only breed with their own subspecies, in order to maintain distinct populations of each. Nevertheless, attempts are made to ensure that each tiger breeds only with one to which it is not closely related, as this helps to maintain genetic diversity. This has been successful, and a survey carried out in 2008 showed that genetic diversity among the captive population of Amur tigers was significantly greater than the genetic diversity among wild Amur tigers.

(a) Explain how natural selection could account for the differences between Amur tigers and Bengal tigers. (5 marks)

(b) (i) Explain the meaning of the term *genetic diversity*. (2 marks)
    (ii) Suggest why the captive population of Amur tigers has a greater genetic diversity than the wild population. (3 marks)
    (iii) Explain why it is desirable for a population to have a reasonably high genetic diversity. (3 marks)

Total: 13 marks

■ ■ ■

Candidate A

(a) It is very cold in Siberia, so it is an advantage for the tigers to have thick fur ✓. The lighter coloured stripes could help them to be camouflaged against the snow.

> ✐ The candidate has correctly identified a feature of the Amur tigers that adapts them for life in a cold climate, but has not explained anything at all about natural selection. 1/5

question

(b) (i) This means all the different alleles of the genes. ✓

📝 A correct description, but needs to go a little further to get the second mark. 1/2

(ii) Maybe the tigers in the wild are all closely related ✓ and they all just inter-breed with their own family ✓. The tigers in captivity have been bred with other unrelated ones. ✓

📝 Although this is not a very strong answer, it does just manage to make three good points and so gets full marks. 3/3

(iii) The more different genes there are, the more the tigers will vary. If the climate changes ✓, then some of them might be able to survive. Or if there is a new disease.

📝 The candidate shows that he/she understands that the value of genetic diversity is the ability to survive in different or changing environments, by means of an example. To get more marks, this idea needs developing further. 1/3

Candidate B

(a) Natural selection means that only the best-adapted animals survive. Amur tigers with genes for thick fur are better insulated ✓, so they keep warmer and are more likely to survive ✓ in a cold climate than tigers with thin fur. So the thick-furred tigers are more likely to reproduce ✓ and pass on their thick-fur alleles ✓ to their offspring. This goes on happening for many generations ✓, until all the tigers have thick fur.

📝 A clear explanation. Another point that could have been made near the beginning of the answer is that there will be natural variation in the tiger population, with some tigers having thicker fur than others. 5/5

(b) (i) All the different alleles ✓ in the gene pool ✓ of a population.

📝 Correct. 2/2

(ii) The tigers in zoos have been part of a captive breeding programme, where everyone makes sure that they only breed with tigers that they are not related to ✓. In the wild, tigers have very large territories so they don't meet each other very often ✓. So the tigers that mate together may all be descended from just a few ✓ older tigers that always lived there and so they all have similar alleles.

📝 This has the right ideas. The candidate has thought about how tigers probably live in the wild, and has surmised that there is less chance of a tiger meeting and mating with an unrelated animal than there is in zoos. 3/3

(iii) This is so if there is a new disease ✓ then maybe at least some of them will be immune to it and they won't all die. ✓

📝 Correct, but not quite enough for full marks. 2/3

Question 5

(a) The diagrams below show a prokaryotic cell and a plant cell from a leaf.

Prokaryotic cell

Cell from a plant leaf

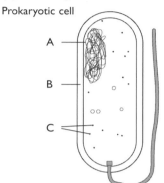

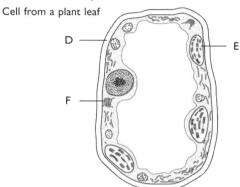

    (i)   **Name the structures labelled A to F.**   (6 marks)

    (ii) **State *two* features of the prokaryotic cell which differ from all eukaryotic cells.**   (2 marks)

    (iii) **State *one* difference between structures B and D.**   (1 mark)

    (iv) **Give the *letter* of the structure which is likely to contain the most magnesium, and outline the role of magnesium in the cell.**   (2 marks)

(b) For much of the twentieth century, all prokaryotes were placed in one kingdom. All other organisms were classified into one of four more kingdoms.

Most classification systems now split the prokaryotes into two domains, and place all other organisms into a third domain.

Outline why this major change in the classification of living organisms has been made.   (3 marks)

Total: 14 marks

■ ■ ■

Candidate A

(a) (i) A chromosome ✓

        B cell wall ✓

        C ribosome ✓

        D cellulose cell wall ✓

        E chlorophyll ✗

        F Golgi apparatus ✓

    e All correct except E, which should be chloroplast. 5/6

(ii) It does not have a nucleus ✓. It does not have cellulose in its cell walls. ✗

🖉 Not all eukaryotic cells have cell walls, so although this second statement is correct it is not an appropriate answer to the question. 1/2

(iii) The cell wall in the bacterium is not made of cellulose. ✓

🖉 Correct. 1/1

(iv) E ✓ because chlorophyll ✓ contains magnesium.

🖉 Correct. 2/2

(b) They found out much more about prokaryotes that they did not know before ✓. Although they look the same, some of them have very different metabolism ✓ so they were divided up into different groups.

🖉 The candidate correctly states that new knowledge has been obtained, and that this relates to the metabolic pathways in the two groups of prokaryotes. 2/3

Candidate B

(a) (i) A loop of DNA ✓

B cell wall ✓

C ribosome ✓

D cell wall ✓

E chloroplast ✓

F Golgi apparatus ✓

🖉 All correct. 6/6

(ii) It has smaller ribosomes ✓ and no nuclear envelope. ✓

🖉 Both correct. 2/2

(iii) The cell wall of a bacterium is made of peptidoglycans ✓, whereas the cell wall of a plant cell is made of cellulose.

🖉 Correct. 1/1

(iv) The nucleus because magnesium is part of spindle fibres. ✗

🖉 Incorrect. 0/2

(b) All prokaryotes have a similar structure as far as we can see with an electron microscope ✓. However, now we know more about their metabolic pathways and some really important differences have been found ✓ between those in Archaea and those in Bacteria ✓, so they have put into two separate domains ✓. All other organisms (which are eukaryotes) have been put into a third domain. ✓

🖉 An excellent answer, which gets the maximum possible number of marks. 3/3

Question 6

Two parents with normal skin and hair colouring had six children, of whom three were albino. Albino people have no colouring in their skin or hair, due to having an inactive form of the enzyme tyrosinase. Tyrosinase is essential for the formation of the brown pigment melanin.

(a) The normal allele of the tyrosinase gene is **A**, and the allele that produces faulty tyrosinase is a.

State the genotypes of the parents and their albino children. (2 marks)

(b) Albinism is a relatively frequent condition in humans, but one of these albino children had a very unusual phenotype. While most of her hair was white, the hair of her eyebrows developed some brown colouring, as did the hair on her hands and lower legs. Genetic analysis suggested that a mutation had occurred in the faulty tyrosinase allele.

Suggest why it is likely that this mutation occurred in the ovaries or testes of the girl's parents, rather than in her own body. (2 marks)

(c) The graph below shows how the activity of normal tyrosinase and tyrosinase taken from the albino girl were affected by temperature.

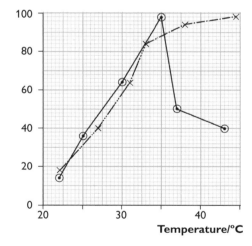

(i) Compare the effects of temperature on normal tyrosinase and the albino girl's tyrosinase. (3 marks)

(ii) Studies on the production and activity of tyrosinase in living cells found that normal tyrosinase leaves the endoplasmic reticulum shortly after it has been made, and accumulates in vesicles in the cytoplasm where it becomes active. However, the tyrosinase in the albino girl's cells only did this at temperatures of 31°C or below. At 37°C, her tyrosinase accumulated in the endoplasmic reticulum.

Use your answer to (i) and the information above to discuss possible explanations for the distribution of colour in the hair on different parts of the albino girl's body.

(4 marks)

Total: 11 marks

■ ■ ■

Candidate A

(a) Aa and aa ✓✓

> 🖉 The candidate has not made clear which genotype refers to the parents and which to the children, but has generously been given the benefit of doubt. 2/2

(b) If it had been in one of her own cells, then only that cell would be affected and not the whole body. ✓

> 🖉 Correct as far as it goes. 1/2

(c) (i) Both enzymes get more active as temperature increases. ✓ The normal enzyme is still getting more active even at 45°C. ✓ The girl's enzyme has an optimum activity at 35°C ✓ and above that it quickly ✗ gets a lot less active.

> 🖉 The answer begins well with a sentence about both enzymes. Two clear distinguishing points are then made. However, the use of the term 'quickly' is inappropriate as there is nothing about time on the graph. 'Steeply' would have been better. 3/3

(ii) Maybe her legs and eyebrows and hands were colder, ✓ like in a Himalayan rabbit. So the enzyme would not work well where it was hotter ✓ and would not make melanin.

> 🖉 This is a difficult question, and the candidate has done well to think of what he/she had learned about the interaction between genes and environment in animal hair colour and recognise that it could relate to this situation. However, the answer does not refer clearly to the information provided, and this needs to be done in order to achieve more marks. 2/4

Candidate B

(a) Parents Aa and Aa. ✓ Albino children aa. ✓

🖉 Correct and clear. 2/2

(b) If it had occurred in her own body, then it would probably be in only one cell ✓ so you wouldn't see the effects in cells in different parts of the body. If it had been in one of the parents, then the mutated gene would have been in the zygote ✓, so when the zygote divided by mitosis the gene would get copied ✓ into every cell in her body.

🖉 Absolutely correct. 2/2

(c) (i) The activity of both enzymes increases as temperature increases from 22°C to 35°C. ✓ However, above that the activity of the girl's enzyme drops really steeply ✓ so it has only 50% activity at 37°C. But the normal enzyme keeps on increasing its activity up to where the graph ends at 45°C ✓. At 38°C it has 97% activity, almost twice as much as for the girl's enzyme. ✓

🖉 A good answer which mentions particular points on the curves and provides a quantitative comparison between the figures for the two enzymes at a particular temperature (38°C). 3/3

(ii) The extremities of the girl's body will be cooler than other parts ✓, so the tyrosinase will be able to work here because according to the graph it can work well up to 35°C ✓. It will also be able get out of the endoplasmic reticulum ✓ in her cells and into the vesicles where it becomes active. This is why the hairs on her hands and legs are darker because the enzyme was able to make melanin there ✓. But in warmer places the enzyme stops working and can't get out of the RER so no melanin is made ✓.

🖉 An excellent answer. The candidate uses both sets of information (from the graph and the description about the endoplasmic reticulum) to provide an explanation linked to what he/she had already learned about the control of hair colour in other situations. 4/4

Sample paper

Question 1

(a) The diagram shows a small part of a cell, as seen using an electron microscope.

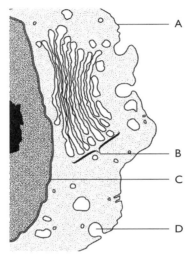

    (i)   Name the parts labelled **A** to **D**.   (4 marks)

    (ii) Describe how part **B** is involved in the formation of extracellular enzymes.

                                                    (3 marks)

(b) Give *two* reasons, other than the presence of part **B**, why the cell in the diagram cannot be a prokaryotic cell.   (2 marks)

                                                  Total: 9 marks

■ ■ ■

Candidate A

(a) (i) A plasma membrane ✓

        B Golgi ✓

        C nucleus ✗

        D phagocyte ✗

    📝 C is the nuclear envelope (or membrane), not the nucleus itself. A phagocyte is a cell — perhaps the candidate is thinking of a phagocytic vesicle. 2/4

(ii) First, the enzymes are made by protein synthesis on the ribosomes. Then they go into the endoplasmic reticulum. Then they are taken ✓ to the Golgi where they are packaged. Then they go in vesicles ✓ to the cell membrane where they are sent out by endocytosis.

🖉 This candidate has not really thought about exactly what the question was asking, and has wasted time writing about events that take place before and after the involvement of the Golgi apparatus. There is, however, a mark for the idea that the Golgi receives proteins that have been in the RER, and another for packaging them into vesicles. 2/3

(b) It has a nucleus ✓. And it has Golgi apparatus. ✗

🖉 The Golgi apparatus is part B, and this has been excluded by the question. 1/2

Candidate B

(a) (i) A cell surface membrane ✓

B Golgi apparatus ✓

C nuclear envelope ✓

D vesicle/endocytosis ✓

🖉 All correct. 4/4

(ii) Proteins made in the RER are transported to the convex face ✓ of the Golgi apparatus in vesicles. The vesicles fuse ✓ with the Golgi and the proteins inside are modified ✓ by adding sugars to make glycoproteins ✓. They are packaged inside membranes ✓ and sent to the cell membrane.

🖉 All correct. 3/3

(b) If it was a prokaryotic cell it wouldn't have a nucleus ✓ and it would have a cell wall. ✓

🖉 Correct. 2/2

Question 2

Linen is made from flax fibres. These are obtained from sclerenchyma fibres associated with the phloem tissue in the stems of flax plants.

(a) The diagram shows a bundle of sclerenchyma fibres.

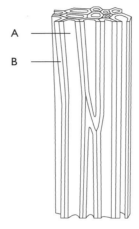

A

B

State the contents of the parts labelled **A** and **B**.   (2 marks)

(b) The diagram below shows a cross section of the stem of a flax plant, indicating the positions of the different tissues.

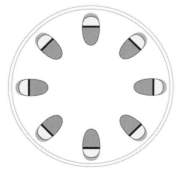

(i) Use a label line and the letter **S** to indicate where the sclerenchyma fibres used to make linen are found.   (1 mark)

(ii) Suggest the function of the sclerenchyma fibres in the stem.   (1 mark)

(c) An investigation was carried out to measure the density and tensile strength of three samples of glass fibres and flax fibres. The results are shown in the table.

Sample	Glass fibre				Flax fibre			
	1	2	3	Mean	1	2	3	Mean
Density/ g dm^{-3}	2.56	2.56	2.55	2.56	1.40	1.41	1.40	1.40
Tensile strength/GPa	1.6	2.3	2.3		0.6	1.5	1.2	

(i) Complete the table by calculating the mean tensile strengths of the glass fibres and the flax fibres. (2 marks)

(ii) Describe how you would find the tensile strength of a sample of flax fibres. (4 marks)

(iii) Glass fibres and flax fibres can both be added to plastics to produce a composite material with great strength. Because glass fibres have a greater tensile strength than flax fibres, they produce a stronger material.

Use the data in the table and your own knowledge to suggest two reasons, other than cost, why flax fibres may be preferred to glass fibres when producing composite plastic. (2 marks)

Total: 12 marks

■ ■ ■

Candidate A

(a) A contains nothing ✓, and B contains lignin. ✓

🖉 Both correct. 2/2

(b) (i)

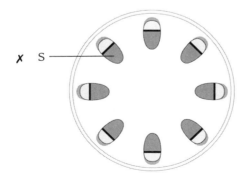

🖉 The candidate has labelled the xylem tissue. 0/1

(ii) Support ✓

🖉 Correct. 1/1

(i)

	Glass fibre				Flax fibre			
Sample	1	2	3	Mean	1	2	3	Mean
Density/ g dm⁻³	2.56	2.56	2.55	2.56	1.40	1.41	1.40	1.40
Tensile strength/GPa	1.6	2.3	2.3	2.067	0.6	1.5	1.2	1.1

           ✗   ✓

🖉 The candidate gets a mark for correctly calculating both means. However, there are too many decimal places in the answer for glass fibre — the measured tensile strength is only to one decimal place and therefore the mean should be, also. 1/2

(ii) Hang the fibres from a support and tie the bottom end to a weight hanger. Put masses on the hanger ✓. Keep putting masses on until the fibre breaks ✓ and then record the results.

🖉 Correct as far as it goes. 2/4

(iii) Making glass uses sand so it might damage the environment more than growing flax plants. ✓ Flax plants are sustainable.

🖉 This is a sensible suggestion. However, the second sentence is really making the same point as the first one. 1/2

Candidate B

(a) A is just air, because all the cell contents have died ✓. B is lignin. ✓

   🖉 Correct. 2/2

(b) (i)

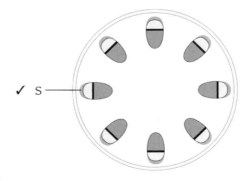

   🖉 Correct. 1/1

(ii) They help to support the stem. ✓

📝 Correct. 1/1

(i)

	Glass fibre				Flax fibre			
Sample	1	2	3	Mean	1	2	3	Mean
Density/ g dm⁻³	2.56	2.56	2.55	2.56	1.40	1.41	1.40	1.40
Tensile strength/GPa	1.6	2.3	2.3	2.1	0.6	1.5	1.2	1.1

📝 Both correct. 2/2

(ii) Tie the fibres tightly to a firm support so they can hang down. Tie the bottom end to a weight hanger. Place a small mass on the hanger, then keep adding masses ✓ until the fibre breaks. Record this mass, and multiply the mass in kg by 10 to find the force in newtons ✓. The maximum force ✓ applied to the fibres before they break ✓ is the tensile strength. (PS in the table the tensile strength is measured in pascals, which is pressure, so they must have measured the area of the fibres and then worked out force over area.)

📝 A clear and entirely correct answer. The candidate has obviously done this experiment and measured the force in newtons. He/she has noticed that this is not the unit given in the table, and has tried to explain it — this was not necessary but it does show he/she has really thought about the data provided. 4/4

(iii) The glass fibres are denser so they would be heavier, so if you were making something that needed to be lightweight then flax would be better ✓. Using flax might be more sustainable than using glass.

📝 One good point is made, and the candidate is on the way to making a second, but needs to say a little more, by explaining why using flax would be more sustainable. 1/2

Question 3

(a) The diagram below shows part of a flower just before fertilisation takes place.

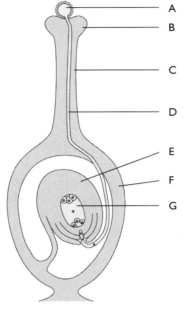

(i) Give the letter of each of these structures.

embryo sac   ovule   stigma   (3 marks)

(ii) On the diagram, draw label lines to each of the following structures and label them.

pollen tube nucleus   female gamete nucleus   (2 marks)

(b) Describe how fertilisation will occur in this flower.   (4 marks)

(c) Explain the importance of fertilisation in sexual reproduction.   (4 marks)

Total: 13 marks

■ ■ ■

Candidate A

(a) (i) Embryo sac G ✓, ovule F ✗, stigma B ✓

📝 Two correct. 2/3

(ii)

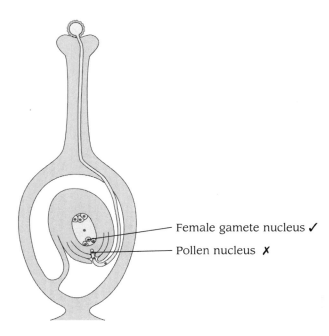

Female gamete nucleus ✓

Pollen nucleus ✗

🖉 The candidate has wrongly labelled one of the male nuclei instead of the tube nucleus, but the female gamete nucleus is correct. 1/2

(b) The male nucleus will fuse with the female nucleus ✓ and this will make a zygote ✓ which will develop into an embryo.

🖉 Two correct statements. The point about the embryo does not relate to the question, because it goes beyond the process of fertilisation. The candidate has forgotten about the fusion of the other male nucleus with the endosperm nucleus. 2/4

(c) Fertilisation means two haploid cells fuse to form a diploid cell ✓, so the new plant will have the right number of chromosomes in its cells. Fertilisation also produces variation.

🖉 The idea of maintenance of chromosome number from generation to generation is correct. The statement about variation is too vague to earn any marks. 1/4

Candidate B
(a) (i) Embryo sac G ✓, ovule E ✓, stigma B ✓

🖉 All correct. 3/3

question

(ii)

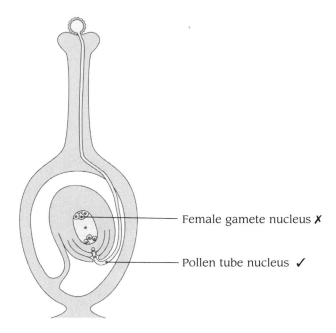

Female gamete nucleus ✗

Pollen tube nucleus ✓

 The pollen tube nucleus is correct, but the female gamete nucleus is wrong — it is the one at the end closest to the micropyle (the gap in the integuments around the ovule). 1/2

(b) One of the male nuclei fuses with the female nucleus ✓. They were both haploid so the zygote is diploid ✓. The other male nucleus fuses with the diploid nucleus ✓ in the middle of the embryo sac, producing a triploid nucleus ✓.

 All correct. 4/4

(c) Sexual reproduction involves haploid gametes. Fertilisation is the fusion of the nuclei of two gametes ✓. This forms a diploid zygote ✓. So fertilisation makes sure the new organism has the correct number of chromosomes ✓. It is also important in producing genetic variation ✓, because any male gamete can fuse with any female gamete and because they will have different alleles ✓ the zygote can end up with different combinations of alleles from its parents ✓.

 An excellent answer. 4/4

Question 4

(a) The diagrams show a cell in various stages of the cell cycle.

A 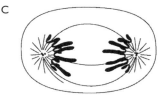   B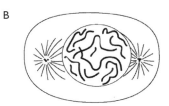

C 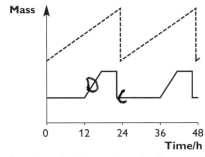   D

Name the stage represented by each diagram, and arrange them in
the correct sequence. (5 marks)

(b) Describe the role of spindle fibres (microtubules) in mitosis. (3 marks)

(c) The graph below shows the changes in the mass of **DNA** and total cell
mass during two cell cycles. Different vertical scales are used for the
two lines.

Cell mass -------

DNA mass ———

(i) On the graph, write the letter D to indicate a time at which **DNA**
replication is taking place. (1 mark)

(ii) On the graph, write the letter C to indicate a time at which
cytokinesis is taking place. (1 mark)

(d) Mitosis produces new cells that are genetically identical to the parent
cell. However, meiosis produces new cells that are genetically different.

(i) Describe the roles of mitosis in living organisms. (2 marks)

(ii) Outline the ways in which meiosis produces genetic variation. (3 marks)

Total: 15 marks

question

Candidate A

(a) A metaphase ✓, B prophase ✓, C telophase ✓, D anaphase ✓

> The candidate has named each stage correctly, but has not arranged them in the correct order. 4/5

(b) The spindle fibres pull the chromatids to opposite ends of the cell. ✓

> This is correct, but there is not enough here for three marks. 1/3

(c)

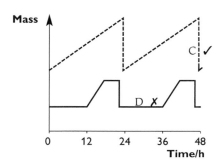

> Cytokinesis is identified correctly, but DNA replication is not. 1/2

(d) (i) Mitosis is used in growth and repair. ✓

> This is correct, but not a good enough answer for 2 marks at AS. 1/2

(ii) Crossing over and independent assortment. ✓

> The candidate has identified the two processes that result in genetic variation in meiosis, but has not said anything about either of them. So he/she earns just 1 mark for the two names. 1/3

Candidate B

(a) B prophase ✓, A metaphase ✓, D anaphase ✓ C telophase ✓ ✓

> All identified correctly, and in the right order. 5/5

(b) Spindle fibres are made by the centrioles. They latch on to the centromeres ✓ of the chromosomes and help them line up on the equator ✓. Then they pull ✓ on the centromeres so they come apart and they pull the chromatids ✓ to opposite ends of the cell in anaphase.

> A good answer. 3/3

(c)

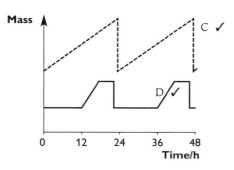

🅔 Both correct. 2/2

(d) (i) Mitosis is used for growth. When a cell divides, the new cell gets exactly the same chromosomes as the original cell, which is what you want for growth ✓.

🅔 There is really only one point made here. The question has already stated that mitosis produces genetically identical cells, so there is no credit for stating this in the answer. The candidate could have said more — for example, stem cells could have been mentioned in relation to growth. There is no mention of asexual reproduction, which is another important role of mitosis. 1/2

(ii) Independent assortment, where the chromosomes can line up any way on the equator in metaphase 1 ✓. Crossing over, where chromatids of homologous chromosomes break and rejoin during prophase ✓.

🅔 The statement about independent assortment needs to make clear that it is the *pairs* of chromosomes that can 'line up any way'. Neither description says anything about alleles — for example, that during crossing over the alleles on one chromosome may be different from those on another, so that crossing over leads to different combinations of alleles on the chromosomes. 2/3

Question 5

(a) The diagram shows a sperm cell.

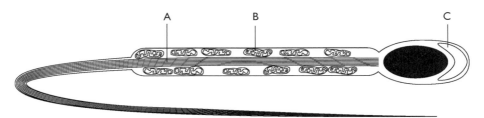

Describe the roles of each of the following parts in the events immediately preceding fertilisation of a female gamete.

(i) part A (1 mark)

(ii) part B (3 marks)

(iii) part C (2 marks)

(b) There are a small number of stem cells in the testes of mice, which are normally able to produce only sperm cells. In 2007, a way was found to 'reprogram' the stem cells so that they become pluripotent.

(i) Explain the meaning of each of the following terms:
   stem cell
   pluripotent (3 marks)

(ii) The stem cells were 'reprogrammed' by exposing them to various chemicals. Suggest what the 'reprogramming' is likely to cause to happen inside the cell. (2 marks)

(iii) It is hoped that the use of stem cells may eventually become routine medical therapy for several serious diseases. Discuss the reasons why being able to use pluripotent stem cells derived from adult testes may be preferable to using embryonic stem cells for this purpose. (5 marks)

Total: 16 marks

■ ■ ■

Candidate A

(a) (i) This helps the sperm to swim.

    ✎ This is true, but a little bit more information is needed to earn a mark. 0/1

    (ii) This is a mitochondrion where respiration ✓ happens. This provides energy ✓ for the sperm cell to be able to swim ✓.

    ✎ This is just enough to get all 3 available marks. 3/3

(iii) This is the acrosome and it contains enzymes to digest a pathway into the egg. ✓

📝 There is no credit for naming the acrosome because the question asks about its function, not its name. 1/2

(b) (i) A stem cell is a cell that can divide to produce other cells. ✓ Pluripotent means it is very strong and able to produce a large number of other cells.

📝 The definition of a stem cell gives only just enough information to get 1 mark. The definition of pluripotent is not correct. 1/3

(ii) The organelles inside the cell would change.

📝 This is not enough for a mark. 0/2

(iii) It would mean no embryos will have to be killed to get the stem cells. ✓ It will be much easier and cheaper to get stem cells from a man's testes.

📝 The first sentence makes a good point. The second needs to be developed a little more before it gets a mark — for example, by explaining why it would be 'easier' or 'cheaper'. 1/5

Candidate B
(a) (i) This is a microtubule and they provide the movement ✓ that makes the tail lash from side to side.

📝 Correct. 1/1

(ii) This is a mitochondrion. Aerobic respiration ✓ happens here, making ATP ✓ that is the sperm cell's source of energy.

📝 Two correct and relevant points. The candidate could have got a third mark by saying what the sperm cell uses energy for. 2/3

(iii) This is the acrosome. When the sperm cell meets an egg, the acrosome bursts open and lets out its hydrolytic ✓ enzymes ✓. These help to break down the zona pallisade ✗ around the egg so the sperm nucleus can get in and fertilise it.

📝 There is a mark for knowing that this organelle contains enzymes, and another for the fact that these enzymes are hydrolytic. The reference to digesting the zona pellucida would also have been worth a mark, but the spelling is wrong (it looks like 'palisade' as in 'palisade cell'). Usually, spelling does not matter, but when it means the word could be confused with something else then the candidate won't be credited. In this case it does not matter, because the answer has already scored the maximum number of marks. 2/2

(b) (i) A stem cell is an undifferentiated ✓ cell that can divide to produce new cells which can become specialised ✓. A pluripotent stem cell is one that can produce lots of different kinds ✓ of specialised cells.

☑ Clearly explained. 3/3

(ii) They probably switched on different sets of genes. ✓ When a cell gets specialised, certain sets of genes are switched on and others are switched off. So reprogramming might change these so different ones are switched on and off.

☑ This is a difficult question, and the candidate has made a good attempt at it. However, after the first sentence the answer really just repeats the same idea twice more. To get a second mark, the answer could have explained that in the reprogrammed stem cells *all* of the genes would become capable of being switched on or off, so that whatever set is needed to produce any specialised type of cell would become available. 1/2

(iii) It would be good because it is difficult to get stem cells from embryos because there aren't many available embryos ✓ and they might have to be killed ✓ which many people disapprove of. There are lots of testes and it wouldn't do any real harm ✓ to a man to have some cells taken from his testes.

☑ Quite a good answer. A little more needs to be made of the ethical objections to using embryos, in order to get a mark for that. Other points that could have been made include the fact that if the person to be treated was male, then his own testes could provide the stem cells. When the stem cells were placed into his body, it would accept them because they would be his own cells. If cells from an embryo were used, his immune system would probably reject them unless he was treated with immunosuppressant drugs. 3/5

Question 6

The Irish Threatened Plant Genebank was set up in 1994 with the aim
of collecting and storing seeds from Ireland's rare and endangered plant
species. The natural habitat of many of these species is under threat.

For each species represented in the bank, seeds are separated into active
and base collections. The active collection contains seeds that are available
for immediate use, which could be for reintroduction into the wild, or for
germination to produce new plants and therefore new seeds. The base
collection is left untouched. Some of the base collection is kept in Ireland,
and some is kept at seed banks in other parts of the world.

(a) Suggest why seed banks separate stored seeds into active and base
   collections.   (2 marks)

In 2001, an investigation was carried out into the effect of long-term
storage on the ability of the seeds to germinate. Fifteen species were
tested. In each case, 100 seeds were tested. It was not possible to use
more because in many cases this was the largest number that could be
spared from the seed bank. In most cases, the germination rate of the
seeds had already been tested when they were first collected in 1994, so
a comparison was possible with the germination rates in 2001 after
7 years of storage.

The graphs show the results for two species, *Asparagus officinalis* and
Sanguisorba officinalis.

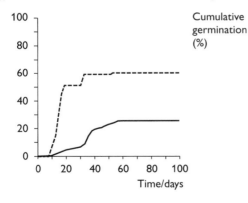

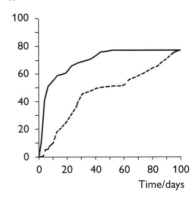

(b) (i) **Compare the germination rates of stored and fresh seeds of**
Sanguisorba officinalis. (3 marks)

(ii) **Compare the effect of storage on the germination rates of**
Sanguisorba officinalis and Asparagus officinalis. (3 marks)

(c) **It has been suggested that species stored as seeds in seed banks have**
different selection pressures acting on them compared with the same
species living in the wild.

(i) **Explain why the selection pressures in a seed bank and in the wild**
are likely to be different. (2 marks)

(ii) **Discuss the possible harmful effects of these differences, and**
suggest how they could be minimised. (5 marks)

Total: 15 marks

■ ■ ■

Candidate A

(a) So they always have some spare.

📝 Not enough for a mark. 0/2

(b) (i) The stored ones germinated better than the fresh ones. The stored ones go up
more quickly than the fresh ones. But they all end up at the same place, about
80% ✓.

📝 This answer loses out by poor wording, and not being clear enough about exactly
what is being described. The word 'better' in the first sentence could mean that
the seeds germinated more quickly, or that more of them germinated, so the
candidate needs to clarify this. 'Go up more quickly' is also not clearly related to
germination. The last sentence is quite generously given a mark for the idea that
eventually about 80% of the seeds in each batch germinated. 1/3

(ii) The <u>Sanguisorba</u> seeds germinated better when they had been stored, but the
<u>Asparagus</u> seeds germinated better when they were fresh. Storing the
<u>Sanguisorba</u> seeds made them germinate faster, but the <u>Asparagus</u> seeds
germinated slower. ✓

📝 Again, poor wording means that this answer only gets 1 mark. The word 'better'
is used in the first sentence and, as has been explained above, this is not a good
word to use in this context. One mark is given for the idea that storage caused
slower germination in Asparagus but faster germination in Sanguisorba. 1/3

(c) (i) The conditions in which the seeds grow might be different in the seed bank
from in the wild.

📝 This is not quite correct as seeds do not grow. Growth only happens after germination, so it is seedlings and plants that grow. The candidate needs to think more carefully about what happens to seeds in a seed bank. 0/2

(ii) The seeds could be grown in conditions like those in the wild.

📝 Again, this hasn't been clearly thought out. 0/5

Candidate B

(a) Having active collections is good because it means there are seeds available that can be used for something. But you must always keep some seeds in storage, because the whole point of a seed bank is that it stores seeds and these need to be kept safe so they don't get destroyed ✓. If all of them got used for growing plants, then perhaps the plants would die ✓ and you wouldn't have any seeds left.

📝 This is not very well expressed, but the right ideas are there. 2/2

(b) (i) The stored seeds germinated much faster ✓ than the fresh ones. By 10 days, about 60% of the stored seeds had germinated, but only about 8% ✓ of the fresh ones. By 50 days, all of the stored seeds that were going to germinate (about 80%) had germinated. It took 100 days for 80% of the fresh seeds to germinate. ✓ We can't tell if any more would have germinated after that because the line is still going up when the graph stops. ✓

📝 Clear comparative points have been made about the speed at which germination happened, and also about the maximum percentage of seeds that germinated. 3/3

(ii) Storage seemed to help the germination for Sanguisorba, but it made it worse for Asparagus. For Asparagus, storage made it germinate slower, but it germinated faster for Sanguisorba. ✓ And for Asparagus only about 30% of the stored seeds germinated compared with 60% of the fresh seeds, ✓ but with Sanguisorba about the same percentage of seeds germinated for both fresh and stored ✓.

📝 A good answer, which again makes clear comparisons and discusses both the speed of germination and the percentage of seeds that eventually germinated. 3/3

(c) (i) In the seed bank, the seeds are just stored. So the ones that survive are the ones that are best at surviving in those conditions as dormant seeds. ✓ In the wild, the plants have to be adapted to grow in their habitat ✓, so maybe they have to have long roots or big leaves or whatever. In the seed bank, that doesn't matter. So you might get seeds that are really good at surviving in a seed bank but when they germinate they produce plants that aren't very good at surviving in the wild.

question

 This is a good answer which really does answer the question, but it could perhaps have been written a little bit more carefully and kept shorter. 2/2

(ii) You could keep on collecting fresh seeds from plants in the wild ✓, and only storing them for a little while before replacing them with new ones ✓. If you had to store seeds for a long time, you could keep germinating some of them ✓ and growing them in conditions like in the wild ✓ and then collect fresh seeds from the ones that grew best ✓.

 This is a really good answer to a tricky question. The candidate has made several sensible suggestions, including storing the seeds for a shorter time and periodically exposing the plants to natural conditions where the 'normal' selection pressures will operate. 5/5